Forged

in the Flames of

Agony

and

Laughter

Experiences and lessons learned from a
regular dude combat veteran who's lived
an extraordinary life. So far.

BRYAN C. HOOD

DEDICATION

I dedicate this book to my wife and kids. Thank you so much for your grace during my times of struggle. You guys mean everything to me. To my parents, thank you so much for always supporting me and my hair-brained ideas. You guys rock!! I also dedicate this book to my combat veteran brothers and sisters. My hope is to reach many who need to be pulled from the dark valley and be encouraged to live an awesome life you deserve.

Brotherhood is forged in the flames of agony and laughter.

I've forgotten more than I can remember.

The main reason for writing this book is legacy building. Words we speak fade with time. Recorded words last an eternity. These are my personal beliefs and stories I want my family to know for generations.

I believe we have one shot on this rock to create our story. You can create and build your legacy or do nothing. It's all about the dash between your birth and the death date on your tombstone.

What will people say about you?

Go out into the world and be epic!

LANGUAGE DISCLAIMER

You will see some foul language in this book. My aim is to keep this book as real as the stories I tell. The language is for context. Don't judge.

"I write because I don't know what I think until I read what I say."[1]

— Flannery O'Connor

---

[1] Goodreads. "Flannery O'Connor Quotes."

"In "Forged", Bryan Hood shares his remarkable journey - as a warrior, father, son, and man of faith - with depth, purpose and authenticity. A great read for anyone who is lost, struggling, or in need of inspiration and truth."

-Josh Goldberg, author of "Struggle Well".

PREFACE

What Will Be Your Story?

I started writing this in January of 2018 while sitting in my favorite chair, drinking coffee and staring up at the mountaintop of 2019. A year ago, after climbing the summit of 2017, I was walking in the valley between the majestic mountains of life God had pulled from the earth for me to enjoy. Doing things the hard way was how I survived, how I learned. I had a feeling inside of me that thrived in the daily struggle of getting by. I didn't like people and could barely stand my own kids at times. I was an unhappy grump. I was mad at God for the injuries I had sustained that would not allow me to continue the job that had given me so much joy. Why would He take that from me? The "strength through struggle" saying that would become my credo was foreign to me, and quite honestly, just really didn't make sense.

As far back as I can remember, I've always enjoyed putting myself through some sort of physical punishment. When I was in junior high, I would punch cassette tape cases into rubble until my fists were bloody. I once branded myself with a cigarette lighter and still have the scar to show it. I also branded my right shoulder with a metal pipe. While sitting in journalism class in high school, I found a piece of glass and proceeded to cut lines in my left arm. The scars are still there. Throughout my twenties and thirties, I'd do things like ridiculously heavy and long ruck marches around my town or in the state forest just to feel the pain in my knees, shoulders and back. During my ten-year CrossFit experience, some of the workouts I did were unattainable, but I'd push myself to complete them anyway—falling to the floor in a puddle of sweat afterwards. Looking back, maybe it was because I didn't feel worthy of peace. One thing I knew was that I wasn't happy, and something had to change in my life.

Being a combat veteran, I was big on purpose and identity. I identified as a freedom fighter and a CrossFit gym owner. I prided myself on looking across the field at the people I swore to serve and defend. But I was also rotting on the inside. The thought of smiling, genuinely telling someone I loved them, hugging someone, or heaven forbid, crying in front of people made me laugh. No way was that gonna happen. Sure, I wanted to help and serve people, but I think it was more for my own sense of accomplishment.

Constantly seeking out a quick fix to make me happy, I used to turn to projects to occupy my time. I once built a ginormous tree house in the woods behind my house "for my kids." Weeks later, I was asked to build one for a friend. One that I built even better than my own. It was not easy to pull those walls fifteen feet into the air on my own. I'm not the type of person to ask for help anyway. It goes back to the struggle that I had always relied on. I was absorbed with struggling for my own self-gratification. But I realized that those moments in solitude made me happy. I was able to spend time visiting with my heavenly Father in conversation.

I look back on the emotional hell I went through in February 2017 at Boulder Crest Retreat (BCR), a combat veteran retreat in Virginia. I was like an onion having my layers peeled back, exposing me for who I truly was. I wore a lie. I realized I was portraying someone I was not. It was exhausting, and it made me unhappy.

After I returned home, I was like Keanu Reeves in The Matrix after he was reborn. I was excited and anxious to learn but just had no real direction. I started to write a bit, but the main thing I started to do was to listen. Hearing people tell their own stories. People are fascinating, and people yearn to be heard. Listening to other warriors publicly tell their stories helped to make me realize that weakness is being afraid to be transparent and real. Weakness is putting up a front. Listening to civilians helped me see the big picture that is we are all human and we all struggle. We all have feelings and we all have a past. It really helped me to blend the two parties.

I can't believe how much I grew over the course of that year. I've become more sympathetic towards people. My faith in God has grown immensely. But one thing I still struggle with is listening to what I hear. I tend to dismiss "gut feelings" or the Holy Spirit speaking to me. But the more I do that, the less I hear it. When we tend to do our own thing and make our own path based on our own human understanding, things go badly. About halfway through the year, I began to listen to that voice more and things started to happen. More positive things. I still struggle with getting uncomfortable, but I'm getting better at it.

See, people want instant gratification. A quick fix. Those don't exist. Sure, you can take a pill for the headache, but it will not cure the cause of the headache. You have to get to the root of the problem. Admitting faults, becoming real and getting uncomfortable are your only saving graces.

The term "experience more" has become very meaningful to me. So many people fear stepping out of the bubble of comfort. Saying "yes" to something new, like a career for example, is very scary. But there is a reason it was offered to you.

Joseph Campbell, mythologist, writer, and lecturer, is known for saying that "the cave you fear to enter holds the treasure you seek." I have to remind myself of sayings like that. In my personal experience, when I entered my personal cave of introducing myself and meeting people who were nothing like me, really stepping out of my comfort zone, I found people who would become great friends. I also found a passion for reaching out to serve in a much more peaceful capacity rather than a combat zone or military environment.

I climbed the proverbial mountain in 2017 and conquered it. Standing here, staring at the mountain of the New Year, I am better prepared for the climb. I believe the climb to the top will happen much faster than last year due to the gear I have to climb it and the party I'll be climbing it with. I can't express how excited I am to conquer this mountain and look back on it a year from today.

Let's make this year our "YES" year. What will your story be?

"Get uncomfortable. Get right. Win the day."

— Greg "Coach" Morin

CONTENTS

ACKNOWLEDGMENTS

I want to thank Ken and Julia Falke. They founded Boulder Crest Retreat in Bluemont, Virginia. The staff consisted of Kevin Sakaki, Suzi Landolphi, Dusty Baxley, Josh Goldberg, Greg Morin and Paul Downs. Attending BCR introduced me to Post Traumatic Growth. My life has absolutely turned around 180 degrees from who I used to be. I will forever be indebted to the Falkes and the staff at Boulder Crest Retreat for helping me to turn my heart back online.

To my brothers I attended with: Randal, Danny, Tod, Bill, and Justin. Thank you for helping me realize who I needed to become. Love you guys.

Warrior PATHH 022

I would also like to thank Alora Boerner. Without her help editing this book it would probably be all over the place. I appreciate your patience with me.

Chapter 1: Getting Started

Optimism vs Realism. What's the Difference?

Optimism is hoping, and realism is the action that is really happening right now. Hoping for the best requires nothing but candy cane and lollipop dreams, and we are often disappointed when reality does not play out the way that we dreamed. You can control your reality and the way you respond to life by being decisive. As you'll find out, I've been the butt of the reality joke too many times in life. I'm not saying I'm a pessimist or a negative person; I've just seen how many situations play out.

It's hard to tell people to be more realistic. Unfortunately, it usually takes some set of circumstances or an event to make them become that way. It goes back to learning from experience. And I had that first learning experience in Kuwait:

In 1996, I was in Kuwait on a two-month deployment. We were supposed to be there from April to June. No big deal. I knew my sister's wedding was planned for August 10, so I had plenty of time to go on my deployment, redeploy and make it to her wedding. The beginning of June rolled around and we had already begun to prep for redeployment: cleaning gear, vehicles, etc. I don't remember the exact date, but one morning we had our normal formation. However, this time the Commander spoke. He informed us that this guy north of Kuwait, Saddam Hussein, was getting ornery and they needed us to stay put for a "Presence Mission" for sixty days. I thought, *WHAT! I can't!! I have my sister's wedding to attend.* Guess what? I didn't get home until August 14 and missed the wedding.

This is one of the times I've been sorely let down by circumstances out of my control. I remember some before, and many after, but this one was a game changer for me. This is when you could say I "woke up," meaning that I looked at the world differently, without rose colored glasses, as Anthony De Mello talks about in his book *Awareness*:

> You want freedom? Here it is: Drop your false ideas. See through people. If you see through yourself, you will see through everyone. Then you will love them. Otherwise, you spend the whole time grappling with your wrong notions of them, with your illusions that are constantly crashing against reality.[2]

From that point on, I became a disciple of realism.

Realistic thinking is knowing that things don't and won't always go as planned. Realistic thinkers tend to just chill and let things work themselves out because they know that, in due time, things will come around. But you also have to take action. You can control your reality. You control it by choosing your attitude and how you respond to a given situation. You rejoice when things go your way, but on the flip side, if they don't, the letdown is not so hard. In my opinion, hoping really does nothing but set you up to get

---

[2] De Mello. *Awareness*.

your feelings hurt, if there is no action that goes with it.

Sometimes, my wife gets twisted because of the way I am. My realistic thinking sometimes makes me a bit of a buzzkill—the whole "hope for the best but plan for the worst" thing. She gets excited about upcoming events or vacations and I'm like "Meh, we'll see." For example, we're leaving for a trip soon. A trip we've been really looking forward to. She asked me the other night, "Aren't you excited?" I told her, "I'll get excited when we're wheels up on the plane." I kind of deflated her joy balloon. But she knows my experiences have taught me to avoid disappointment by going with the flow.

"Waking up" is a liberating feeling. Being realistic has really helped me to control my stress and anger. This mindset has helped me to be more patient when waiting on hold or standing in a line. I pray for things and hope that God will do His good works and bless my prayers. Having woken up to reality and how life really works has also helped me to realize that His plan is better than mine and not to get my little feelings hurt when something I pray for doesn't come to fruition.

Bottom line: whatever hand you're dealt is your reality. What you make of it is your decision. Your choice. You can be dumbfounded, complain, argue and bring others down with you, *or* you can make the decision to thrive and think of any situation realistically. We combat vets are pretty good at this stuff. We can sleep on the desert or jungle floor, eat nasty food, sweat, bleed and deal with bugs. We don't like it, but it's the reality of the situation. In the same way, when we are back home, we have to change our focus from the negative and "be all we can be."

Be that light for the weak minded and lost.

Why Life Isn't Going Your Way

Soldiers are very judgmental. It's a learned trait, and we sometimes don't know how to turn it off. We "git shit done," meaning make a decision and move out. We are trained to make judgment calls based on the information we hear, see, smell, whatever. There is not a lot of the heart involved in the process. We are very black or white. Do *something*! So, when we see people post stuff on social media about how they can't find a job, can't do this or that, we judge. I, personally, have been working very hard to break this after twenty-five years of service. Life isn't hard; it's hard work. If you're not willing to put in the work, yep, life will continue to be hard. Only you can make the change.

I've been trying to wrap my mind around issues some of my buddies have shared about being "broke." Not physically, but in the wallet. It truly baffles me when a buddy will call or message me to catch up and they tell me how bad life is for them. I try not to offer the "quick fix," but it usually heads that direction. Most the time, the issue is money. They can't pay their rent, house payment or other bills. They go on to talk about how there are no jobs or people just aren't willing to pay them what they are worth.

I look at things like this: if you are thirty years old or older and can't afford to spend $500 on something you need or want, more than likely, you're the problem. There's gonna come a point when you just have to wonder, *Maybe it's me*. There is a whole world out there with thousands of ways to make money. Call it poor decision making or budgeting, but I think it's deeper than that.

If you can relate to my buddies with financial problems, then you probably fall into one of these four categories:

1. **You're lazy**. If you're looking for rainbows and butterflies and the river of fudge to swim in, you're gonna get your feelings hurt. The most successful people in this world are those people who are willing to work the hardest. Notice I didn't say wealthiest. You may have a million-dollar idea, but unless you're willing to sweat and bleed over it, it will always remain just that: an idea. Long hours and, most importantly, an unyielding level of commitment is what will get you there. Nothing really worth going after is easy. Roll up your sleeves and dig in.

2. **You're lacking experience or education**. People go to college or some sort of "higher education" and expect to go into that field and make it big. This is a "rose colored glasses" way of seeing the world. Whether you exit high school, college or do like me and take the G.E.D. route, your learning does not stop there. You *have* to seek self-improvement. You should *always* strive to

learn something new, even if you're not interested in the subject matter. Lack of experience/education will place you in the long line of the unemployed.

3. **You're blaming everything and everyone but yourself**. People fail to accept responsibility for their failures or setbacks. Blaming the world, the government, your ex, your neighbor, your parents, your teachers, etc., seems to be the norm. As a Sergeant in the Army, I was taught to "seek responsibility and accept responsibility for your actions." That's a leadership trait. Not everyone can be a leader, no matter how many try. People would be amazed at how things would turn around if they would just stop, look in the mirror and say, "I screwed up and it's my fault. I'm going to change right now." Seek responsibility and people will seek you. Learn to humble yourself and accept responsibility for your failures, setbacks and mistakes. BE-KNOW-DO.

4. **You lack motivation and a positive mindset**. If you don't have a reason for what you are doing or what you want in life, then you'll never get there. I used to tell

my gym members, "If you think you can't, you probably won't." I would watch someone walk up to the bar to pull their all-time record deadlift and say, "I don't know about this." I'd simply tell them, "I do, you won't make that lift." Then I'd tell them to step away, and I would give them the good ol' Bryan Hood version of the *Rocky* motivational speech. I'd help them switch their mindset by telling them to close their eyes and visualize their goal. Not many people are going to visualize failure. They'd visualize the lift, and I'd tell them, "You've already completed the lift in your head. Now do it for real." Yes, it'll be hard. And if you're using a "hook grip," it'll hurt. You take the pain with the success. Every great warrior has felt pain on their journey to greatness. That's why you have to earn it.

Number 4 is probably the most important one to me. It truly baffles me and makes me want to slap someone or shake them, seeing how little they think of themselves and how unworthy they think they are. Every single human being is capable of greatness and success in life, no matter how you define success.

So here's my advice for you to think about today: quit blaming the world and start gaining self-confidence.

Where you are right now is your fault. No one else's. If you sit in your pajamas all day playing Xbox, developing Cheeto fingers, and complaining because no one has called you back for a job, it's your fault. Where you are right now is not due to being born into poverty, being beaten by your parents, being abused by your uncle or being born with your looks. It's due to your mindset, choices and lack of action, persistence and commitment. You are only limited by what you think you are capable of accomplishing. If you want to live a hard life, roger that, enjoy. Just don't blame anyone but yourself and don't spread your disease of failure.

"So, Bryan, what do I do now?" Take a step down a new path. One step at a time, one foot in front of the other. It's not easy. The phrase "fake it 'til you make it" has so much truth to it. When the world pushes at you, you push back. Never settle for mediocrity. You were designed for greatness! Prove it. Learn something today. Learn new skills to make yourself more marketable, more attractive. I love the movie *The Pursuit of Happyness*. Remember these words: Competence, Candor,

Courage and Commitment. All winners in life display those traits. That's what it takes to crush life.

You know one of the greatest things about living in America? Free enterprise. When you can take a rock and write "Pet Rock" on it and sell it, you're in the right place. Sure, you can go work for someone else, there's nothing wrong with that. It's just not for me. I choose to dictate my own schedule, what I wear, where I go. I will allow no one to tell me what I'm worth. No one will place a cap on what I'm capable of doing or making.

Choices: What Our Future Holds For Us

Tony Robbins, author, philanthropist and life coach, said, "If I'd had the mother I wanted, I wouldn't be the man I am proud to be."[3] What is he talking about? Due to his horrific childhood, many times at fear for his life from his mother, he has evolved into what many attempt to become. He was so driven by fear, anger and optimism that, among the chaos of his daily life, he had enough clarity to make decisions in his life to lead him to a

---

[3] Robbins. "Tony Robbins – Blame Them."

billion dollar empire. Another successful man, Swiss psychiatrist Carl Jung said, "I'm not what happened to me, I am what I choose to become."[4] Jung went on to be influential in the fields of psychiatry, anthropology, archaeology, literature, philosophy, and religious studies.[5]

It's about creating change, folks. The ability to have clarity amidst chaos will enable you to make thoughtful decisions. Tom Brady is probably the master of this. If you watch him, immediately after the snap, it seems that he has an eternity to make a decision. During the chaos of the noise from the crowd, teammates smashing into the opponents, being chased like prey, he still makes a sound and precise decision, and then executes his decision with precision. Clarity in the midst of chaos. It's really a beautiful thing.

How does this help you? Create space to think, for starters. Tom Brady has his linemen to help him create space, to take a moment to think. In that moment of confrontation, you can create space as well. Don't react immediately.

As soldiers, we've been taught our entire

---

[4] Goodreads. "Carl Jung Quotes."
[5] Fordham. "Carl Jung."

career to react. React to indirect fire, react to ambush, react to NBC attack, etc. Not one CST (Common Skills Task) says to "respond" or to use our heart and mind to develop a response. Taking too much time to think could have gotten us killed in the military, so we had to react immediately. But that training has wired us in such a way that it seems almost impossible to change. A guy takes your parking spot, so you react by pulling up next to him and yelling at him through an open window. Or worse yet, you yank him out through the driver's window and beat him.

In situations like this, it's best to create space to think. If a guy takes your parking spot, stop, think and wonder to yourself why he may have chosen that action. Think, "Maybe he needs to park closer than me because he just had a surgery" or "Maybe he has a sick child at home and needs medicine." We have the choice on how we respond to any situation.

The future? You are what you repeatedly do. "I'm a combat vet, so I'm a tough son of a bitch." "I hate civilians cause they're stupid." "Men who haven't served are wussies." We can, and should, change that perception. We can choose to be happy or bitter old people. We can choose how we want to live our lives and what we want our lives to be. The most important factor is the *courage* piece. Are you bold enough to make that change?

The old adage of "fake it 'til you make it" holds some truth. We have made and continue to make choices daily. Now we must live with them. We choose how our life is lived in front of us. We can't change how life was lived behind us. We combat veterans tend to feel like we have no purpose and we're just waiting for the next fight. What to do, what to do? We can still choose to thrive regardless of the lull we have in this firefight we call life.

Take the meaning behind the story of the labyrinth. Warriors who were sons, brothers, husbands would enter the labyrinth just prior to marching off to combat. In the center of it, they would set down their identity to emerge from the labyrinth as warriors prepared for battle. Upon their return from battle, they entered the labyrinth as a warrior. In the center, they would set their combat experience on the ground, leaving it there and emerge from the labyrinth as sons, brothers, husbands once again. Many modern-day warriors have not done that. We still continue to carry the burdens of our war experience with us, no matter how long it's been since we fought. That clashes with our identity as citizens of our society, functioning as sons, brothers, husbands.

Therein lies the problem. Combat vets playing combat, looking for the next fight, but finding nothing. So, we create chaos of our own. Be it drugs, alcohol, crime. What I urge combat vets to do is pause, create space and be Tom Brady. Combat veterans are masters of making tough decisions quickly and under extreme pressure during chaotic circumstances. So, why not do it now? We can do this with our children, our spouses, our neighbors and our fellow countrymen and women. We can be Tony Robbins and be successful despite what our past has branded onto us. Our experiences make us the great people we are today. We are battle-proven, battle-hardened survivors. We have demonstrated that we can rise against the odds and be successful. It boils down to our choice. The choice to thrive and live or drown and die. What will you choose to become?

Opportunity Abounds!

In my walk through life, I see opportunities

every day. Maybe it's the way I'm hardwired, I don't know. I'm more of a "yes" man than a "no" man. I don't want to be eighty or ninety years old and look back on my life and say, "I wish I would've." Living conservatively is not in me. I have a hard-coded set of morals and values that I will not compromise. That being said, I'm down for whatever.

It almost makes my skin crawl to the point I want to scream when someone is afforded an opportunity and they say no. Mythologist, writer and lecturer Joseph Campbell said, "The cave you fear to enter holds the treasure you seek."[6] Many, *many* folks are fine with mediocrity. I am not. It's like owning a Corvette and never breaking the speed limit. Owning an airplane and never letting it leave the ground. Buying a house on the lake and never even getting near the water. What's the point? We as humans have free will and intellect to make decisions to do amazing things. Why limit ourselves?

"A bit of advice given to a young Native American at the time of his initiation: As you go the way of life, you will see a great chasm. Jump. It is not as

---

[6] Goodreads. "Joseph Campbell Quotes."

wide as you think."[7]

— Joseph Campbell

I'm no grand old wizard on a mountain top, but at forty-three I've learned some things in life. One of those things is to take chances! You have to break the mold of the norm to truly reach your goals. Many people are just comfortable doing life like they've always done. World travel? It baffles me why more people wouldn't want to do it. They see these pictures of exotic places in faraway lands and think, "Man, I'd love to be there and see that, but it's just too expensive, and I really don't have the time." With that attitude, you'll never truly live. You're an excuse maker, and in your world, in your mind, that's OK. You're OK with settling. We are capable of so much more.

Think about this analogy from Rabbi Dr. Abraham Twerski of growth and stress:

> The lobster is a soft, mushy animal that lives inside of a rigid shell. That rigid shell does not expand. Well, how can the lobster grow? Well, as the lobster grows, that shell becomes very confining, and the lobster

---

[7] Goodreads. "Joseph Campbell Quotes."

feels itself under pressure and uncomfortable. It goes under a rock formation to protect itself from predatory fish, casts off the shell and produces a new one. Well, eventually that shell becomes very uncomfortable as it grows…back under the rocks. The lobster repeats this numerous times. The stimulus for the lobster to be able to grow is that it feels uncomfortable. Now, if lobsters had doctors, they would never grow because as soon as the lobster feels uncomfortable, it goes to the doctor, gets a Valium, gets a Percocet, feels fine. Never casts off his shell. So, what we have to realize is that times of stress are also times that are signals for growth. And if we use adversity properly, we can grow through adversity.[8]

When those people finally do make that trip to that faraway place, they say things like, "It was the most incredible experience. It was more than I could've imagined. The smell and sounds were amazing!" Then they see what they almost missed out on because of their hesitation and attitude of

---

[8] Mindfulness 360. "'What We Can Learn."

settling. Our children will watch us and more than likely emulate us as they grow. Do you want your children to experience the fullest life possible? I know I do, and it's my choice to give them those opportunities and vision casting while I can.

"So what if that opportunity was missed? I'm gonna be dead someday. Does it really matter if I took that opportunity? I can't take it to the grave." I'll tell you what! Legacy. How do you plan to ever inspire anyone, like your children or peers, if you have no experiences to share with them? About three years ago, I took my oldest son on a mission trip to Guatemala. We had an amazing time, and I know that he'll never forget it as he talks about it often. The opportunity was offered to me to go, and I said "yes" even though I was hesitant because it was a "mission trip." Turning to my son and offering him the opportunity was the true reward. Since then, I've gone on another mission trip to the Amazon in Brazil and have found that the opportunity offered on that trip was the realization of a passion to offer the chance to other people who cannot afford the experience.

Opportunists are hopeful. You may have a friend on their death bed who may need to feel some hope. Who are you to give that to them if you're not a hopeful opportunist? Take chances in life, folks. Live! We only have a short amount of time on this rock. If someone presents you with an opportunity, seize it! If you continually pass on opportunities, people will stop offering them to you. It's because you've created a pattern of "no." Don't be that person. Take risks, step out of your comfort zone. You must break free of your mold to grow.

How Hungry Are You?

One thing that I find unique about "my people," veterans, is that we are visionaries. You know what "Joes" do when they are sitting around in the back of a Howitzer, in a fighting position at NTC, in the motor pool or back in Supply? They think stuff up.

When I was in Iraq, one of the guys in my unit was a "carny" growing up. His name is Jones, and his parents were carnival people. We spent hours sitting in Humvees just talking about it because his stories were fascinating. (That's one of the great things about the military. You meet all sorts of people from all walks of life.) Jones was telling us stories, and we were asking questions. We asked what the head carny does with all the money. He told us he didn't put it in the bank but just stashed it in different places. The head carny Jones remembered was a bad person; he was crooked. We all kinda looked at one other and said, "Why don't we do a hit?" So we began to mission plan how this would go down—everything from surveillance and recon to location, time, equipment needed, logistical support, plan A-Z, exit plan, and any follow-on missions. We spent hours talking about this. Then we decided we'd pitch the story to Quentin Tarantino to make a movie instead of actually doing it.

Point is, soldiers are visionaries and planners, and we all have a Ph.D. in GSD (Getting Shit Done).

Some of the world's most successful leaders are military men and women:

- Johnson & Johnson CEO: Alex Gorsky
- Proctor and Gamble CEO: Robert A. McDonald
- Walgreens CEO: James A. Skinner
- Viacom CEO: Sumner Redstone
- Foot Locker CEO: Ken Hicks

- General Motors CEO: Daniel Akerson
- Verizon CEO: Lowell McAdam
- FedEx CEO: Frederick W. Smith[9]

See, we have a unique set of skills and experiences. Our minds are creative and artistic. There's an old saying, "improvise, adapt and overcome." That's one reason why vets are the problem solvers in relationships. When my wife comes to me about an issue or a problem, I go into "fix it" mode. Service members, typically, can plan and execute missions. The Army's definition of leadership is "the process of influencing others to accomplish a mission by providing purpose, direction and motivation." That is so ingrained in me due to the many Soldier of the Month and Promotion Boards I've had to attend. There is so much truth there, though. Think about it. You have to have a "why." Why are you doing what you're doing, and what is the intended outcome? Your direction is critical because it will determine how you're going to go about it. That's the planning and execution piece. Lastly, nothing will ever get done without motivation. Motivation can come in many

---

[9] Lockie. "15 Fortune 500 CEOs."

different forms, be it financial, time, freedom, health, happiness, selfless service and helping others just to name a few.

Some people are so hungry to get a job working for someone else. If you're that hungry, be the person who hires other people because the empire you created has outgrown you. If you like taking orders from someone else, being told where to be and when, or you like following the crowd, by all means, proceed. Not me, man. I march to the beat of my own drum. I prefer to beat brush and create my own path, to create my own legacy for my family and children. When life pushes at me, I push back. You'll have to kill me to stop me. If there is something you want to do, do it! Don't *ever* quit no matter what people may say or think. It's the extraordinary people who step away from the herd who do extraordinary things.

Be legendary and start planning and creating your own empire today.

The Past Is Behind You for a Reason

When we are young, we start out in a rear-facing car seat. As we grow older, we progress into the forward-facing car seat and booster. After the booster, we're given a little more freedom to sit in the seat like a big boy. Then, we're finally able to ride in the front. By this time, we understand quite a bit about cars. We know how to get them moving, stop them, start them, etc. The pinnacle day comes when we're finally able to drive them—think turning eighteen. Since the time we first rode in the car, we were being taught by our parents, our family, whoever. Then, we're by ourselves, no more parents to hover over us. But we've taken their lessons with us. Those lessons are what have molded us. If your parents were slow, cautious drivers, there's a good chance you will be, too.

Now, imagine you have a Ferrari, or whatever car you'd love to have. Some people will hold the keys to their Ferrari in their hand and just open the garage and look at the car, admire it and go back inside. Some people may actually go out and sit in it and maybe fire it up. That's as close to the edge as they want to be. People like me? Well…I'm ready to drive! The Ferrari is life. You can look at it and do nothing. You can sit in the seat and ride in it. Or you can drive it! It's yours, and you are ultimately responsible for what happens to it. You control it.

The past is behind you part? Oh yeah. The Ferrari has one giant windshield and a small rearview mirror. You can drive the car unsuccessfully by staring in the rearview mirror, or you can look ahead through the windshield. I've heard former military guys say things like, "I'm a SEAL," "I'm a Ranger," "I'm a Marine." Well, you were. The problem with that way of thinking is that people continue to wear that identity, and they have issues living in the NOW and creating a new identity. It's what you did, it's what happened, it's who you were. It's not who you are today. You don't hear grown men saying they're a football player when they only played in high school. The past is history. Watch this, HIS-STORY.

People who were abused also have trouble separating the past from the present. "I'm worthless." "I'm lazy." "This is the best it's ever going to be." "I'm a victim." These things do not define who you are today. You choose who you are and who you want to be. What happened to you is history. Stop living in the past, stop driving your Ferrari staring in the rearview mirror. Cause you know what? If you live in the past, if you stare at that mirror, you're going to crash. That crash could be subtle or catastrophic. Every day we wake up, we are writing history with every breath we take. Look ahead and create your path.

It's OK to reflect on the past. The past tells us where we've been and where we're going. Just reflect and don't get stuck on it. This is a very common issue with combat vets. They get stuck playing "remember when" and wish they were back in the thick of it. That time is gone and behind you. Those experiences are what made you the person you are today. Good or bad. I recommend going with the good and discarding the bad. We can't change our past, but we can write our future. If you believe it, you can be it. Set your mind on what and who you want to be and what you want to be doing. Tell yourself who you are every day. Speak your goals as if they've already happened and you're living in that achievement now.

The River

This past summer, my oldest son and I went kayaking. During that float, I told him about "The River." He has decided not to go to college, and that's totally fine with me. I did, however, tell him he needed to do *something*. He began to tell me about all the bad luck he's had this year and how he's struggling. I smiled and gave him this analogy:

Son, life is a river. It flows straight ahead, meanders back and forth. Sometimes it's fast and sometimes it's slow. You act according to the current conditions. Sometimes there may be an obstacle. You have to continue to move, so you have to navigate that obstacle. It may be a fallen tree or dry land. Regardless, you have to take action. There are also dangers on the river. Snakes, rapids, waterfalls, and bridges all pose dangers. Be prepared the best you can and be aware. If life isn't going your way, you may want to sit and do nothing. Like any river, it's going to continue to move. Like it or not. One day, you're going to wake up and be thirty and wonder where the past ten years went. You can enjoy the river of life. Make the most of it and learn from it. Or you can sit and do nothing. The river is going to continue to move. You can never go back. You may want to turn around and paddle back into the past. It's behind you for a reason. Make memories and make good decisions. If you need help navigating rough waters on the river, I'm here. I will traverse the river with you and guide you through the rough waters. Why? Because I've been there. I've floated the river of life and am still floating it. When I need help, I ask someone more experienced than me to help. It's OK and wise to ask for guidance. I love ya.

Purpose and Hope

When people would ask me, in reference to risky adventures, "Why do you keep doing those things? Why do you keep pushing yourself"? I simply reply, "Cause I ain't dead yet." See, I believe in continuing to push as long as I have breath in my lungs—physically, spiritually, emotionally and financially. I mean, you'll never see a hearse pulling a U-Haul behind it. You can't take anything with you, but you can build up what will be left behind. It's all about legacy building and becoming a better you. I think the one thing that drives me is a saying I heard at church not long ago. The speaker said, "You ain't dead yet cause God ain't done with you." Man! That's it!! I talked to my wife about that after. I mean, that really made sense to me. It gave me hope!

Purpose

I've had some pretty interesting experiences in my life, experiences where I should've died. I've also talked to angels on two separate occasions. Check out my YouTube channel (www.youtube.com/Hoodlm13b) to see the video of me telling those stories. I don't tell many people about those experiences for fear of sounding like a weirdo, but it's true. As I've aged, I've come to believe that there is truly a reason I'm alive. In the past year, I've come to realize the reason why. God ain't done yet. Now, you may not be a believer, but this still pertains to you. Whatever it is you believe in, God ain't done with you. There *is* a reason you still exist and are still alive and reading this right now. I walk by faith and not sight. That's not easy. I truly believe the best is yet to come in life. That, my friends, gives way to hope.

Hope

I've thought a lot over the years about purpose, my reason for still being here. Heck, even when I was younger I thought about this. I think purpose is something many people think about, and knowing our purpose helps us become expert guides in life. As we age, we experience events. Nietzsche said, "That which does not kill us makes us stronger."[10] Experiences make us stronger physically, mentally, emotionally and spiritually. We all face adversity and challenges. When we overcome those, we become stronger.

As a combat veteran, having served in many combat zones from the Balkans to the Middle East, I've seen and experienced a lot. Trying to make sense of those experiences at the time was a lost cause. I just kept putting one foot in front of the other until the hardship was over. Lao Tzu said, "The journey of a thousand miles begins with one step." That's how we walk through struggle. When we overcome that struggle, we become a better person, thus, making us a prime candidate to walk someone else through that same struggle, being a guide to them. We all have purpose, and knowing that purpose should give you hope.

George Washington Carver said, "Where there is no vision, there is no hope."[11] He's right, you know. You have to have vision. People will say, "I just don't know what it is I want to do." What excites you? What drives you? What makes you happy? What makes you feel accomplished?

---

[10] Goodreads. "Friedrich Nietzsche Quotes."
[11] AZquotes. "George Washington Carver Quote."

For me, it's helping people. That truly makes me feel good. My love language is words of affirmation. That being said, when I help someone, they usually express their thankfulness, and that makes me feel good. So, do the math. Helping people + Receiving appreciation = My happiness.

How

I figure since we all have gifts and skills we're good at, we could tap into those and use those for good. Right? I like to talk to people via written, verbal or visual communication. That's the key word right there, *communication*. How do you know what your gift is or what you're good at?

1. What have people told you you're good at doing?
2. What do you enjoy doing?
3. Would you do it for free?

Hopefully, all three of those answers are the same or at least have an intersection point. Whatever the answer is, that's what you should be pursuing. Knowing that should give you hope now that you know you have purpose and a gift.

Change In Life Is Your Decision. Own It.

I have a hard time staying in bed in the morning. My mind races and the thoughts begin to flood my mind. I toss and I turn. I kick the sheets off of me, then pull them up to my neck. I start to get angry, then I throw the sheets back with a *whoosh*, sit straight up then spin to the right. Once my feet are on the floor, I begin to move like the house is on fire. Sometimes my wife says, "Come back to bed. You need to get some rest!" "Nope," I say, "Time to get to work." Whether it's reading something to fuel my brain, firing up the 'puter, or just looking out the window and seeing the world, I'm excited. Like a kid on Christmas morning.

I didn't used to be like this. Now, due to new ventures in my life and a rebirth of action, I am ready to slay dragons from the get-go. See, I'm very creative. I'm a self-starter but not much of a self-finisher. I'm the ultimate "Good Idea Fairy." If I had millions of dollars, I'd have patents on equipment, copyrights on words and about twenty side businesses. I have trouble prioritizing because everything is priority *numero uno*.

I loathe failure, and I'm pretty hard on myself when and if I do fail. I do know, however, in the right context that failure is good. If we always succeed, we rarely gain wisdom. I have tried and failed at many things, mainly because I'm not really scared of anything, except for failure. So, I'm a risk taker, be it physical, monetary, emotional. I know our life on this rock is short. The clock is ticking, and things need to happen. I don't always know how to make things happen, and I just jump in head first and start to do something. As I mentioned, I have a Ph.D. in GSD (Getting Shit Done). I have a responsibility to teach my kids about hard work and not being afraid to get their hands dirty.

I had been trying to find out who I was and where I was going for the past six months. What is my purpose? I was very frustrated. Being a combat veteran is neat and all, but the problem is that when you are "over there," you are a god in your own mind. You experience things that the normal person cannot comprehend, and you deal with it. You are subjected to constant danger and you thrive and live. When you come home, you're "normal" like everyone else, and your "god status" is gone. How are we supposed to get that rush, make a difference and be important again? I have searched for that for years, trying to grasp what it is I'm supposed to be doing and who I am.

I recently got involved in "one of those Multi-Level Marketing things." It cracks me up when people say that. A Multi-Level Marketing (MLM) company is no different from any other corporation. "Only the people at the top make all the money" is what people whine about. You think the mail room boy is gonna make more than the CEO? Exactly like any other company, you have to work your way up. Some people are ambitious enough and have the work ethic to actually do it. Others are the ones who quit after a month or three because they're not millionaires with the car that was promised.

People who do not know will call an MLM a "pyramid scheme." A pyramid scheme is an illegal investment scam based on a hierarchical setup. By law, if there is no real buyer or product, that is a pyramid scheme. New recruits make up the base of the pyramid and provide the funding, or so-called returns, the earlier investors/recruits above them receive. A pyramid scheme does not involve the selling of products. An example of a legal pyramid scheme is Social Security.

I am absolutely pumped about the direction

I'm going with it. My company has given me purpose and direction. I wholeheartedly believe in the products, which is why I take them daily to help with the physical pain due to degeneration of this weathered body. There has been a change in mission since retiring. My heart is still for helping those who are unable to help themselves—not helping those who choose not to help themselves—and I love sharing the products to help others.

So here I am. I've gone through some experiences recently that have helped me to realign and give me hope in the direction I'm going. The creative side in me is like molten lava. It's hot and running all over the place with no specific path and affecting everything it comes into contact with. I have to act on this. I cannot sit and let this run its course without embracing it. I believe everything happens for a reason. I know that strength comes from struggle.

My pretty extensive knowledge of CrossFit and the methodology translates to everyday life. Like trying to press that bar from your chest at the gym, if you continue to press through, it will make you stronger. Subjecting your mind and body to new challenges is how you get results. Routine is the enemy. You have to have variety in life to grow.

I welcome struggle. I'm not always prepared for it, but I know I can and will make it. I have struggled and continue to struggle today. I work through it. I am motivated to stir change in the life of others. I am motivated to create and share opportunity with others. Some people just don't get it. Those are the people who "settle" and complain about their lives. They fear change but desperately want and need it. I suppose it just hasn't gotten bad enough for them to take that risk to free them from the stagnation in which they live.

Bottom line is this: **BE BOLD!** Take chances, people!! If you complain to me about how you're not happy with your current life, you're broke, your relationship sucks, etc., and if you don't choose to change it, I want to slap the snot out of you in hopes of trying to wake you up. Do something! Take a chance, and take that risk. I often ask people what they wanted to do when they were a kid. They tell me and then proceed to tell me it's not possible now. If you think you can't, you won't. Ever. I know I can and I will. I will brush off the charging bulls of negativity and the naysayers. I choose my own actions, and I will reap the benefits and the experience and knowledge gained from those actions. Be different to make a difference.

Chapter 2: Accountability Friends

Your Tribe

I don't care who you are, everybody needs friends, a tribe. Harvard University has an ongoing study they started in the 1930s called the Grant Study. The goal of the study was to "identify predictors of healthy aging,"[12] and it included four members who ran for the U.S. Senate, one who served in a presidential Cabinet, and one was President John F. Kennedy.[13]

George Vaillant, who directed the study for

---

[12] Wikipedia contributors. "Grant Study."
[13] Shenk. "What Makes Us Happy?"

more than three decades, summarized what they have learned so far, including how alcoholism and your relationships with your parents can affect your success:

> Financial success depends on the warmth of relationships...not intelligence. Those who scored highest on measurements of 'warm relationships' earned an average of $141,000 a year more at their peak salaries (usually between ages 55 and 60). No significant difference in maximum income earned by men with IQs in the 110–115 range and men with IQs higher than 150.[14]

In a nutshell, relationships are important. Real, genuine relationships mean everything. Jim Rohn, motivational speaker and self-help guru, says, "You are the average of the five people you spend the most time with." If you hang with boozers, chances are, you'll be a boozer. If you associate with successful people, chances are, you guessed it, you'll be successful. Choose your friends wisely. These are your closest confidants. They know everything about you, and you know everything about them. There's an old saying in the

---

[14] Wikipedia contributors.

Army: "Army buddies. Trust them with your life but not your money or your wife." Luckily, I've found a few friends that I'd trust in my home, alone with my wife, while she's in the shower. Now those are good friends.

Pruning

This is a fun one! Think of a grapevine or rose bush. If you want it to grow and be healthy, you must prune it and remove the dead or unnecessary leaves. We are much the same. It's important for us to prune people, habits, locations, etc., out of our lives if we want to grow. This could even be as extreme as family members to include spouses. Although it's a necessity, it's not easy to do. Buck up and do it. Down the road, you'll be glad you did. Now, that's not to say that your growth can't be a positive influence on said person(s). Just be aware of the effect it may have on you to reconnect after a period apart. Most times, you'll find that you've grown so much that you now have nothing in common with that person.

I've chosen to prune a few people out of my life, as well as lifestyle choices, because every time I get around those people or participate in those activities, I feel myself reverting back to the way I was. It's not conducive to my personal growth. I also chose to remove myself from the whole "Dysfunctional Veteran" movement. After stepping back and analyzing it, I realized it was counterproductive and kept me in the hate spiral I was in. I stopped attending anything veteran-related for about a year or so. I had to disconnect.

After we've begun our pruning, it's time to fill our "growth tank." This is when you'll want to surround yourself with people, environments and activities that support your new path. That may be joining some sort of group or class. Personally, I've really enjoyed meeting new people. People I wouldn't normally hang out with. With the company I've been working with, I was able to hit a position that rewarded me with a "paid for" car. It's not really paid for, but as long as I continue to produce, they would make the payments. I bought a Nissan 370z Nismo Tech. This sucker is saWEET!

After getting my new-to-me ride, my dad recommended that I join a car club. I thought, *That'd be fun*. After asking around, someone mentioned the local Z Club to me. I joined the club. I've enjoyed the few events I've attended, and I like the time spent in that environment. It makes me feel good. The people are quite a bit different from me. Some of them are a lot younger and can't really see past the tip of their nose, in the whole spectrum of life. The point is, I joined a club where we all have one common interest, the Z car. Other than that, I really have nothing in common with most all of them. What's the takeaway? I've enjoyed meeting new people and getting to know a few of them, getting out of my comfort zone and feeding this new direction in life. Step out, get uncomfortable and meet new people.

Disclosure

This is a very hard thing to do. This is basically stripping yourself down to nothing. No hidden cards tucked up your sleeves. The analogy I was given was "taking a knee and unpacking my ruck." I disclosed things that I had never told anyone. It was very hard and very liberating at the same time. It's important to lay it all out there and talk about it. Once it's out there, there's never a need to revisit it. Move on. It doesn't have to be an in-depth conversation, but it should be recognized. If forgiveness needs to happen, it's done at that time. This all plays into the whole "rearview mirror" story.

In the book *Lessons from the Hanoi Hilton*, the authors discuss the principles that made the American POWs imprisoned at the "Hanoi Hilton" so resilient in captivity. Disclosure was a very critical piece to their survival. When one of the guys would succumb to the torture sessions and give up critical intel, they'd go back to their cell, "get on the wall" and disclose what had happened. Again, this is a very critical piece of personal growth. Having that tribe or someone you can confide in is when this comes into play. Disclosure must happen to move forward, or you risk staying stuck staring in the rearview mirror. Don't do that.

After taking that knee and unpacking my ruck, I felt much lighter. I felt that new possibilities were on the horizon. After spending the week at BCR and returning home, I had no idea what I was going to do. I literally didn't know what to do the first day home. It was like I was a newborn all over again. Releasing the load from the past made me ready to run again. I remember thinking to myself, "Yes! I love people!! I love life!!! What the heck am I going to do?!"

I officially broke the chains of the dark parts of my past. I was able to move forward. I know so many people who are continuing to drudge forward in life carrying that load. They are holding the secrets and dark experiences close to them. They live staring in that proverbial mirror. I've talked to many people about this when they've asked what has changed with me. They just won't let go. No one can help them.

Integrity (Honesty/Transparency)

Integrity is probably one of my most important values. This value is everything when it comes to a person's character. Be honest with others and be the same person everywhere you go. Don't put on your church hat on Sundays, beer drinking hat on Fridays and business hat throughout the week. Be the same person everywhere you go. If not, you stand being called a hypocrite. Many people aren't prepared to hear the truth. Those people only want to hear what they feel they need to hear at a given time. Not me, man. No way. I'll tell you what's on my heart at any given time. So, be careful what you ask me. The most important piece to all of this is to be tactful, be frank. Being an honest person may actually put you on the receiving end of disclosure. It's an honor for someone to trust you like that. The saying, "Say what you mean and mean what you say, but don't say it mean" is so true. Never judge and never make assumptions.

One of the greatest takeaways from my time in the Army is the Army Values. It seemed super cheesy at the time when they handed us those Army Values cards and the dog tag. We were forced to memorize them.

Army Values

<u>Loyalty</u>: Bear true faith and allegiance to the U.S. Constitution, the Army, your unit, and other soldiers.

<u>Duty</u>: Fulfill your obligations.

<u>Respect</u>: Treat people as they should be treated.

<u>Selfless-Service</u>: Put the welfare of the nation, the Army, and your subordinates before your own.

<u>Honor</u>: Live up to all the Army values.

<u>Integrity</u>: Do what's right, legally and morally.

<u>Personal Courage</u>: Face fear, danger, or adversity (Physical or Moral).

Being older now, I realize that having those ingrained in us forced us to always be mindful of them. Those values made me want to be the best Non-Commissioned Officer (Sergeant) I could be. They made me want to be more professional and set *the* example for my subordinates. Once you burn your integrity, you don't have much left. It takes a while to earn it back. Strive to be a person of great character. Be bold and make the hard decisions—right or wrong.

Chapter 3: Daily Routine

Create Successful Daily Habits

Losing is a habit and so is success. Everyone has habits, and they range from biting their fingernails to balancing their checkbook. They are broad. With so many people struggling in life, being on a success campaign deserves some merit.

Over the past year, I've read all sorts of books, watched videos and listened to speakers. A common theme is creating habits that work well for me, being a military-minded person. In the military, our days are very regimented. We work from a training schedule. Over time, the routine activities in that schedule become habit—physical training, for example. After many people leave the military, they tend to carry on the morning routine of doing PT. It's a habit. Not long ago, I sat and thought about all this and decided to come up with my own daily habits. Over time, like Darren Hardy mentions in his book *The Compound Effect*, these subtle changes create profound change.

I strive to start every day the same way, so I created a schedule to win each day! I have this on a whiteboard on the back of my office door:

- 0600-0615 Wake up, make tea, take morning supplements

- 0615-0630 Stretch and reflect

- 0630-0655 Pray and Meditate

- 0655-0705 Write down three things I'm grateful for and positive "I am" affirmations

- 0705-0715 Daily schedule review

- 0715-0745 Read

- 0800 Crush the day!

There you go, two hours in the morning to prep for a successful day. Now, most people will say,

"Must be nice to have all that time to do that stuff, but it's not realistic." I don't have a 9–5 job I go to. I work from home, which was a choice I made years ago. You can too. Life is based on choices that we make or don't make. Take action!

That being said, you can mimic this, but you must make it a priority. You just might have to wake up earlier, which means you may have to go to bed earlier, which means you may have to stop whatever it is you do that is a time and success stealer. Bottom line, your success is dictated by your own actions. Your happiness is dictated by your own choices. I choose to thrive and live a happy life. Sure, there are days that I slip from this morning routine, but that's OK. I know it and pay for it. Sometimes life just happens. I usually try to make up for it somewhere else in the day. My wife knows when I've slipped because she holds me accountable.

One other thing I'll do is listen to Goalcast videos while I'm in the shower. That's probably my #1 way to start off the day. Man, I can't tell you what it does to your soul and your drive, to start out the day listening to people like Mel Robbins, Joel Osteen, Denzel Washington, Les Brown, Jim Rohn, Tony Robbins, scripture, etc. Fill your mind with positive and uplifting information.

You may or may not have noticed that I didn't list anything about checking social media. Garbage in/garbage out. Too many people plug into the Matrix too early in the morning. I *highly* recommend prayer and meditation practice. When I can, I'll walk our trail around our property just talking to God like He's right there with me. He is. So, I'll thank Him, tell Him my issues and what's on my mind, then ask Him for help. Meditation really centers me and prepares me for stresses that will come my way. I'm a work in progress and progress is good! I once read that you should spend the first hour of your day exercising your body and mind. That's why I like to stretch/walk and read. Think about where you want your day to go, and make it happen.

What Is A Healthy Lifestyle?

When relating to Post Traumatic Growth (PTG), I see a resemblance to the "Healthy Living Movement." I believe it encompasses a full spectrum of wellness. The healthy living that my company speaks of primarily relates to nutrition.

Nutrition plays a major role in our overall health, both physical and mental. Dr. Richard Tedeschi has studied this for over thirty years. I am a student of PTG and his work. There are five domains to PTG. They are as follows:

1. Greater Appreciation of Life and Changed Sense of Priorities
2. Warmer, More Intimate Relationships With Others
3. A Greater Sense of Personal Strength
4. Spiritual Development
5. New Possibilities[15]

The Greater Appreciation of Life and Changed Sense of Priorities

This piece not only relates to our own life but to others as well. Going back to my spiritual outlook and how much I've grown in my faith, I understand and know that everyone has a purpose. I don't believe that people were put on this earth to simply exist. Every single person has a purpose and a destiny to fulfill. I also have had a greater appreciation for non-human life as well. I respect

---

[15] Ramos and Leal. "Posttraumatic Growth."

our environment more as well as all plants and animals. Everything we see and have is a gift.

Warmer, More Intimate Relationships With Others

After my pruning stage in life, the relationships I have with people have gotten more intimate. I listen better and am able to show empathy towards others. The time I spend with those close to me is much more enjoyable. It's also liberating that I can be open and real versus wearing a mask to hide my heart and share what's in it.

A Greater Sense of Personal Strength

When a person begins their journey back to the high ground, they must realize and understand how strong they are. It takes strength just to begin the journey. Once I returned to the person I am now, I realized, looking back, how far I've come after realizing how lost I was. My personal strength came from knowing my own past and what I had to do to create change in myself. That involved breaking old habits and separating myself from old behaviors. It also involved opening myself up and letting down my guard, something I didn't want to do but knew was necessary for forward progress. I had to share some things with certain people. I had to humble myself in front of my wife and children.

Spiritual Development

This is one area I feel I've grown the most in. The growth in my spiritual life trickled over and touched every other area. I humbled myself before my God and repented. I gave it all up to Him. From there, I began to listen more intently to His word. Plugging myself into my church by volunteering helped immensely. This took some encouragement from my wife and has paid off more than I could have ever imagined. My life has taken turns on my path that I never thought I'd travel. We've all heard that the Lord works in mysterious ways. Although that saying is not in the Bible, it is very true. Once I gave it up to God in Heaven, my life began to take on a new look. I am also not naïve to think that life is going to be all unicorn farts and lollipops. Living a Christian life is hard and has many challenges. The Apostle Paul tells us in the bible that we will face great challenges and struggles. He was right.

New Possibilities

This domain has been the most fun of the five domains for me. Since I began the walk on my path, I've read so many amazing books and have met so many amazing people. Jumping into the network marketing industry has been the biggest growth possibility for me. I've made many new friends, made some money and have made great strides in my personal development. From those new possibilities, other new ventures have emerged. I never thought I'd ever take the leap to write a book, and here I am pounding the keys to share my story. For some, the new possibilities could be a job or relationship. For me, it's been a strengthening of relationships with those I care about most, new opportunities to serve mankind, new friends, new knowledge and growth on so many levels.

Fear

"It's not that we fear the unknown. You cannot fear something that you do not know. Nobody is afraid of the unknown. What you really fear is loss of the known."[16]

— Anthony De Mello

For those people who are believers in the

---

[16] De Mello. *Awareness.*

Bible, they know that fear is stemmed from original sin. Fear is natural, thanks to Adam and Eve for eating that apple and bringing sin into the world. Fear is in our DNA and cannot be taken out. But fear is not something we should give in to because it is from evil and not good. Giving way to fear, however, is usually easier than fighting it. When we give into fear and let fear win, we are stealing God's opportunity to do something great in our life. We are doubting His ability to show us something new or do something miraculous. As G.K. Chesterton said, "We fear man so much because we fear God so little."[17] Even if you are not a believer, know that fear is natural, but letting fear win is not. Only when we face fear head on do we grow. Read the story about David and Goliath, Benaiah and the lion, etc.

Welcome and accept the good and the bad. Take the easy times with the times of adversity. All of it is there to help us grow and become better. We need the hard times and struggles to make us strong and the easy joyful times for rest and reflection.

Are there costs and benefits of avoiding fear?

---

[17] Goodreads. "G.K. Chesterton Quotes."

Absolutely! Dr. Tom Barrett, expert in the psychology of success, explains the benefits of avoiding fear in his book *Dare to Dream and Work to Win*:

1. Avoidance seems to make the fear diminish.

2. It allows me to experience calm.

3. It allows me to avoid doing what I dislike.

4. It allows me to do something else that is more enjoyable.

5. It allows me to live within my comfort zone.[18]

Dr. Tom Barrett also explains the disadvantages of avoiding fear:

1. **Continued avoidance only makes my fear stronger.**

   Since I fear failure because of my disgust for failure, many times I've avoided even trying certain things. Once I found the courage to face my fear of failure and put myself out there, I amazed myself by overcoming my preconceived notion. For

---

[18] Barrett. *Dare to Dream*.

example, in network marketing, I never imagined myself doing it due to my lack of interest in meeting people who weren't like me. I overcame that fear by just jumping in and giving it my all. I have done well.

2. **Avoidance increases my stress and only camouflages my anxiety.**

Running from something I fear is not natural for me. It makes me angry to even think about it. I have such a passion for being a lion, so the thought of fearing something upsets me. However, there are things I have tried to avoid such as the fear of volunteering at church. Sounds silly, but it's true. Every time we'd attend our church and I saw all the volunteers, I felt myself stirring on the inside because I knew I should humble myself and join the team. I always played it off like I didn't have the time. Not true. For so long, I hung on to this stereotype that church men were weak and volunteers had to be all smiley and mushy. Not true.

3. **Avoidance prevents the growth of my profession.**

When I was a young E4 Specialist in the Army, I avoided attending the promotion board to Sergeant. The thought of having to study scared me to death because I've never been a good test taker. Also, the thought of getting passed over for the promotion scared me. Again, the thought of failure paralyzed me. So, I just avoided it for four years. The average time spent in the rank of E4 was two years. I was finally ordered by my Troop First Sergeant to attend the board. I had the highest score out of everyone attending the board that month.

4. **Avoidance prevents the growth of me as a person.**

I used to think, *Why get close to people when you'll be parting ways in the next few years?* That attitude resulted in me keeping my guard up and avoiding getting close to people, opening up to people and letting them get to know the real me. It wasn't until a couple years ago that I finally began to follow my heart instead of my mind. As a person, I have grown so much more allowing myself to open up and learn to have intimate and more authentic relationships with people instead of surface-deep relationships.

5. **Avoidance sabotages my confidence.**

Joseph Campbell's quote, "The cave you fear to enter holds the treasure you seek"[19] screams in my head nowadays. Being bold, taking chances and saddling up anyway has increased my confidence overall. I've realized how much I have learned from failure and struggle and how much better of a person I've become. I am more confident on a much broader spectrum of life events and opportunities as well as challenges I may face.

6. **Avoiding little fears today will create very real and large fears in the future.**

It's the compound effect, 100%. Small changes today will result in major changes in the future. The more I've become accustomed to something, the easier it has been to go along with it. It's drawing the

---

[19] Goodreads. "Joseph Campbell Quotes."

line in the sand and saying "no more."

7. Avoidance will cost me my dream.

This one is easy to get caught up in. I have avoided fears in the past due to fear of failure only to actually try later in life and be successful, resulting in me wishing I had tried earlier. I've also learned that failure begets wisdom—if you learn from your mistakes.

8. Avoidance will keep me right where I am financially.

I've avoided investing in the past. Two years ago, I decided to jump in and try my hand. Yes, I failed in some areas but succeeded in others and have learned a lot on the path. Today, we are more financially stable than we have ever been.

9. The little things I avoid today will be the big regrets of my future.

We can't change what happened yesterday, be it avoiding an opportunity due to fear of the unknown, fear of failure, etc. It's typical to see others around grow and improve their lives. If only we had jumped on the bandwagon when they did, right? It could be volunteering for an organization, investing, learning or growing a new relationship. We don't want to grow old saying, "I wish I would've."

10. **Trading years and years of future freedom to avoid brief moments of discomfort is a horrific life and business decision.**

That's exactly where we were years ago. Luckily for me, I enjoy learning new things. Those brief moments of discomfort in my life have been counseling with my wife and trusting in God to take care of us financially when writing large checks for tithing and moving houses. We are so much better off, so far, for making those decisions.

"Do the thing you fear most and the death of fear is certain."[20]

— Mark Twain

As you can see, there are more costs to avoiding your fears than there are benefits.

---

[20] Goodreads. "Mark Twain Quotes."

Ultimately, those benefits are only temporary, but the costs are permanent. People have an old record playing in their heads from life experiences, be it from their childhood, past relationships, etc. The negative will continue to play repeatedly until *you* change the record. What are you filling your head with? Who are you surrounding yourself with? How do you start your day? How do you maintain positive thoughts throughout the day? Only you can make the changes necessary to live a happy and fearless life.

"The cave you fear to enter holds the treasure that you seek."[21]

— Joseph Campbell

I was taught a theory about basic emotions and that we are born with three primary emotions: joy, fear, and sadness. Just like primary colors and how they are mixed together to make secondary colors, joy and fear may mix to create a feeling of elation or awe. Fear and sadness will create anger. Face your fears, people. Do what is uncomfortable. Do you want to create a legacy? What will people think and say about you after you're gone? Do you want to be remembered as a coward? No. Roger

---

[21] Goodreads. "Joseph Campbell Quotes."

up! Look your fear in the eye and meet it head-on. You may need assistance to fight through that fear. That's OK. Seek it out from someone who has gone before you and experienced what you're experiencing. In the end, you'll be glad you never settled for mediocrity.

Accepting Struggle as Something Good

We are students of life. Period. The sooner you can accept that the sooner you'll start to be more flexible with the ebb and flow in your daily walk. Lessons to be learned, like opportunity, fly past us each day as we breathe in and breathe out. Probably the most important aspect of learning is knowing that it doesn't just happen. We don't live in the Matrix. For something to really burn into the hard drive between our ears it has to be impactful enough, challenging enough, so that our minds can work out and problem solve so that clarity is given ushering understanding of the problem. That is learning.

We've all heard of struggling, but most really don't understand the necessity for it. You've heard the saying by Henry Ford, "If you always do what you've always done, you'll always get what you've always got,"[22] meaning nothing changes and nothing new comes into your life. It is necessary to be open to new paths, new opportunities, new lessons to be learned. Many people enjoy, too much, the bean bag of comfort. As a believer in Christ, I know that curveballs will be thrown my way. The New Testament talks about refinement, and Job went through a refinement in the Old Testament. No one that I know of, to date, has been challenged as much as Job was. The dude lost literally everything. Not only did he lose everything, his physical health was challenged. In today's world, many people would've tapped out. But Job lived, not exactly happily, knowing that God was in control. He knew that life was temporary and that sometimes you have to walk through a great amount of struggle, while remaining faithful, to learn and reap the inheritance of the Lord.

Today, many people can't even fathom the thought of struggle. The moment that big ol' monster steps foot at the door, people triple lock that door and batten down the hatches. I'd say a small percentage of people are willing to answer

---

[22] Goodreads. "Henry Ford Quotes."

the door, look at Struggle and say, "You ready to party? Let's do this." Those people know that change, positive change, is right around the corner. It's like fighting your way to the top of a mountain. It's not going to be easy. It's going to take a while. You may slip and fall and get tired, hungry and cold. You may even change your mind about half-way up. But those who endure the challenge are the ones who get written about. The ones who inspire the world. The people who leave a legacy for their children, friends and communities. Those are the people others aspire to be like. It's all because they looked at Struggle, chuckled and stepped into the octagon of life to go toe-to-toe, all for the sake of learning and becoming stronger.

I implore with the men of today's society to accept those challenges and rise to the occasion. Our children need men who are willing to get their hands dirty, struggle and learn. Our women are not immune to this. Women struggle as well. When I think of the women in America during the 1940s, I am in awe. For the community of women to "roger up" and take on the challenge of holding down the home front while our men marched off to war is just awe-inspiring. Many veterans' wives are those women today. Women also struggle but usually in different ways than men. Not any easier, just differently. Why? Because we all must grow to become great. You have to struggle to grow! Growth isn't like a pizza to be delivered to you. You don't just pay someone for it. You can read all the self-help books you want, but if you don't put action behind it, nothing will happen. It's the same thing as all the hopeful people joining a gym at the beginning of the year. A very small percentage of them are still there in July or even April or March. Good intentions, right? You have to struggle.

Celebrate when hard times come knocking. The reason most people check out or run is because they don't have an accountability partner or group of people to lean on in times of struggle. They shut people out and try to manage it on their own. Let me know how that works out for ya. On the other hand, you don't always need another human to lean on, but it helps. For me, and many others, I always go to God and pray something along these lines, "Alright, here we go. Time to learn and refine myself. I'm going to need your constant guidance, strength and endurance. Please walk with me and help me to know your will and end result for this trial."

For me, this past year has been

revolutionary in my life. I've said "yes" to direct sales, which was a huge obstacle to overcome for me and is still a challenge, and I've been open to opportunities as they have come my way. I have had to trim the fat on friendships, meaning cutting away those people who bring me down. I've tried to lean more into my support group and my family. My relationship with God is the strongest it's ever been. I still struggle daily. People may not see it, but I do. Refinement is not easy. I stumble but am constantly learning, trying to fine tune who I am and my purpose.

For those who accept struggle, I commend you. It's not easy, but it's worth it. Whether you are struggling with PTSD, feeling like you have no purpose, or having financial, marital, or children struggles, just know that you *can* and *will* make it through. As Friedrich Nietzsche said, "That which does not kill us makes us stronger."

Which One Are You Feeding?

There's a Cherokee story about two wolves, and it serves as an excellent parable:

An old Cherokee is teaching his grandson

about life. "A fight is going on inside me" he said to the boy.

"It is a terrible fight and it is between two wolves. One is evil—he is anger, envy, sorrow, regret, greed, arrogance, self-pity, guild, resentment, inferiority, lies, false pride, superiority, and ego." He continued, "The other is good—he is joy, peace, love, hope, serenity, humility, kindness, benevolence, empathy, generosity, truth, compassion, and faith. The same fight is going on inside you—and inside every other person, too."

The grandson thought about it for a minute and then asked his grandfather, "Which wolf will win?"

The old Cherokee simply replied, "The one you feed."[23]

I had never heard this parable until February 2017. Man, did it resonate within me or what?! I realized that I lived a life of constantly feeding the bad wolf. No wonder I was so miserable. At the time I thought I was "5 by 5"

---

[23] First People. "Two Wolves."

(meaning good to go). I would've liked to think I was feeding the good wolf, but as I look at those attributes above, I can honestly say that I wasn't feeding a single one of those things.

So, which one are you feeding?

It wasn't until this was all laid out in front of me and my own struggles were dissected that I realized that I had the choice to move in a new direction. I chose hope. I didn't realize that I was as bad as I was. I thought I was pretty normal, given the life I had lived. Being a combat vet, I used that as my excuse to pretty much be a jerk to everyone, including my wife and kids. I will say that the feeling of liberation from that person I was to the person I am now is almost unexplainable. It's been a tough journey but one that gets easier every day.

The point I want to get across is that if you are where I used to be, you're in luck. They say that you have to have a breakdown to have a breakthrough. I tell people rock bottom is a good place to be because that's what makes a great foundation. From there, you learn and build up what you want to see through the vision that you have cast for yourself. You can truly do and be whatever the heck you want. If you cast that vision and think about it daily, you will arrive at that destination. You have to believe it to be. It's not easy and there are skills I use daily to help me on my journey. As Jocko Willink and Leif Babin talk about in *Extreme Ownership*, "Own our successes and failures. Lead our own lives."[24] Belief is so very powerful and so is knowing that no one can choose our decisions. We own our choices and actions.

Aim High to Achieve Goals

I talk to a lot of people on a daily basis. I truly do love listening to people's stories and learning about those individuals. I usually like to ask people what their goals are. Where they plan to be in a year, five years or even twenty years from now. It's amazing the responses I get. In business, I'll hear someone say, "I'd like to get three new clients in the next six months." Now, this really depends on the person, but if that is that person's goal, they will typically not hit that goal. Why? They set the bar too low; either the time or number is off.

If I am going to shoot an 800m target using

---

[24] Willink and Babin. *Extreme Ownership*.

a rifle chambered in .308, there are some factors that will come into play. We'll take crosswinds out of the equation for this example and only take distance into consideration. If the rifle is sighted in at 100m and I set the center of the reticle center mass on the 800m target, dirt will fly in front of the target. Why? Because I have momentum and the most power/energy at the beginning. But as time and distance increase, velocity will drop. Pulling the trigger on a new venture or idea is the same as pulling the trigger on that rifle. Max power and energy once you set in motion. As time goes by, momentum will decrease.

If that 800m target is a six-month target, much like trying to hit that steel target, I have to set my sights higher to hit it. We call that "holdover." The angle of the barrel has to rise to maximize my trajectory. A .308 round will fall over 50in at just 500 yards. Can you imagine how much it falls at 800m? You have to aim high for the bullet to drop and hit the target.

You have to set realistic but uncomfortable goals to hit your intended goal. In my business, my goal is three to five new customers each week. Some weeks I may only gain one and some I may gain eight but I still keep my sights on that three to five. Don't underestimate yourselves, people. Set high goals and aim high to hit those targets. You have to get uncomfortable to be successful.

Passion and Dream Catching

I'm big on setting goals. I often ask people, "What did you want to be when you were a little kid? Why don't you do it?" Too many people look at that dream and passion as inconceivable, like it's too far-fetched and could never happen. Me? I've lived my dream. When I was a small boy, all I ever wanted to do was travel the world and carry a gun. Be a soldier. Hunt bad guys and get paid for it. Well, I've done that. I could die peacefully now. But God has more in store for me. I'm not sure what it is, but I'm working on it.

If you have a dream or passion, why aren't you pursuing it? What's stopping you? People? Society? Family? Money, or lack thereof? The old saying, "If you put your mind to it, you can accomplish anything" is so true. I explained to my daughter that she was at the base of the mountain looking up at the top thinking, "Holy cow! That is so far up there." And I'm sitting on the top saying,

"Come on up! The view is beautiful!" She just laughed. I told her that I had climbed many mountains. Some I didn't want to but had/needed to, and they are all possible to summit and overcome.

When I was in high school, I went on an Outward Bound trip in Leadville, Colorado. It was the 14-Day Alpine Mountaineering Course. Years later, I found out that Outward Bound was considered a program for "troubled youths." Oh well. That trip truly did change my life, and lessons from that trip stick with me to this day. Tahoe Roland, God rest his soul, was the lead instructor. One evening, he pointed up to the top of a mountain and said, "Tomorrow, we're going to climb that mountain and camp on the other side." I said, "No way! There's no way I'm gonna be able to climb up that mountain with this backpack on." I weighed about 120 pounds at the time, and the pack I was carrying weighed almost half my weight. He laughed and said to me, "Bryan, do you ever have any problems or issues in life?" I said, "Yeah." Then he said, "Think of that mountain like a problem in life that you have to overcome. The *only* way you're gonna be able to climb to the top of that mountain is by putting your head down and putting one foot in front of the other until you're at the top. Don't look at the top of the mountain and be overwhelmed by the size or height. Just look down and keep moving forward. There will be some switchbacks and some actual hand-over-hand climbing. We'll have to use ropes and equipment and it's going to be very hard. But we're going to do it. You're going to do it." I just stood there and thought, "OK, I trust this guy. He's a really cool dude, too. He's climbed Everest, the Matterhorn, and every other giant mountain in the world. Let's do this." You know the end of the story: we did it. The feeling of accomplishment was such a high to me. Now, I try to apply that in my life. Problems, dreams, etc., no matter how big or small, are all conquerable.

If you have a dream or passion, pursue it. Do your due diligence: read, study and research. You can do anything if you put your mind to it. You have to make a choice and decide your attitude. You may have to ditch friends, family or anyone who may be an anchor in your life. Do it. Of course, me being a Christian guy, pray about it. Ask God to walk with you and guide you through your climb. Chase your dreams. Do want you wanted to do when you were a kid. We grow through life's challenges.

Willingness to Be Independent

Relying on external forces to provide for us can lead to disappointment, much like expectations lead to hurt feelings. Being independent basically means being able to provide for ourselves in a multitude of ways. In other words, the lack of independence reduces your survivability, in general.

With advances in technology and living in the modern world, so many things are presented to us on a golden platter. That means we don't have to work as hard as we once did to receive what we need. Gone are the days of plowing fields or riding twenty miles into town once a week for supplies. Nowadays, everything is instant and seamless. Well, for the most part. If it's not seamless, it's usually not that hard to fix. Many people rely on others to get things done. Many people also rely on others to provide their hard-earned pay.

I am an advocate for learning skills and learning to be independent. When the dust settles, it's just you. When it really boils down to it, no one cares for you and your family as much as you do. Independence is a gift that so many people just give away freely. Why? Because being a loner is not easy. You eat what you kill. In many developing countries, if you do not have money to buy or the means to acquire food, you simply starve. In America, we have programs to thwart that. If you have no money you apply for welfare; if you have no food, there are many places to help. This allows people to simply do nothing and skate by in life. Wrong answer!

According to Lifehack, there are eleven reasons why you need to be more independent:

1. It boosts your self-confidence and self-esteem.

2. It decreases the burden you place on family, friends, and society.

3. It turns you into an asset to help other people.

4. It enhances your reputation among friends and colleagues.

5. It leads to financial freedom because you are skilled and capable.

6. It gives you social independence and dexterity.

7. It makes you physically capable of caring for yourself and others.

8. It fills you with a sense of joy and happiness that can come from no other source.

9. It places you in a position to be an innovator with independent thought.

10. It makes you mobile rather than confined within your community.

11. It sets you up for further progress and self-sufficiency.[25]

How do we regain our independence? Learn skills and be bold. Traditional labor skills are a dying art. We need skilled laborers to build, repair and do the arduous work that many Americans are not willing to do. That's why those jobs pay so much. Many people are too scared to take that leap of faith and do something on their own because they lack the know-how and/or direction.

---

[25] Hammond. "11 Reasons Why."

By design, humans are the embodiment of self-awareness. Our brains are constantly working to learn and be creative. Our brains are masters of learning the "how" of things. We are born to be creative. That's why so many children enjoy building, drawing, coloring, making sounds, etc. As we grow older, the tools of the modern-day begin to slip in and steal that creativity from us. Never rob a child of the opportunity to be creative and independent. In the heart of man burns a desire to be free and adventurous, to take a risk and overcome. It's only when people see an obstacle, a mountain that intimidates them, that through a learned reaction, they shy away from the challenge. Boldness is dying. The opportunity you've been waiting for, that "big break," is usually right in front of you, but you are choosing to let fear win. You are not being bold. You can Google anything and find out how to do it. There are people making rockets in their backyard and launching themselves into our atmosphere because they desire to do something bold and courageous.

Being creative, or having knowledge of a need that others can capitalize on, usually dies with the person who had the idea and never takes action. It's easy to talk about an idea or how you would do something, but it's a whole nother thing to take action. That's where most people stop. It's the fear of taking action, the what ifs, that stunts people and extinguishes the fire in their soul. You must learn to be independent. It is so important to have your own "thing."

When it comes to business and making money, it's the people at the top of their industry who chose to go against the grain and proved the naysayers wrong. They chose to remove themselves from the mainstream ideology and stand on their own. That's not to say they didn't find others who were like them to embark upon the journey with. I'm just saying that if you have a desire to do something great, let nothing stop you. Seek out like-minded people. Associate yourself with people you want to be like, those who are doing things you desire to do.

I always ask people, when beginning a new adventure, "What do you feel you have to bring to the table?" In other words, what do you have to offer that will be beneficial to the overall goal? We all have gifts. Go on a journey to uncover and use those gifts. Be bold and choose to step out from the herd. Yes, it's scary but well worth the experience and opportunity to grow and be great. You can still be part of a society and still belong, but don't be afraid to chase your dreams. Ask questions, and don't just take things at face value. Challenge what you hear or see. Find a tribe of people who are like-minded in what you desire so you can learn together. Being independent will reward you the most financially and spiritually. We were not created as part of a "lot" of people like parts on an assembly line. We are all unique, and it's our duty to maintain that uniqueness and use it to prosper.

Wake Up and Be a Lion

Over the past few months, I've been doing some major restructuring in my life. I've changed my social activities, who I surround myself with, who I strive to emulate, what I read, what I watch and how I live life daily. I don't watch sports cause I feel it's a waste of time. I don't pay much attention to the news because most of it is negative. These changes have been good. Not easy, but good. I still struggle just about daily. Struggle is good, though. When you hit rock bottom, you are set on the greatest foundation on which to grow.

How are you living your life? Do people

seek you out for advice? Are you being that someone that others may try to emulate? Are you happy every night when your head hits your pillow? If not, what are you doing to change it? Do you have long-term goals? Are you seeking greatness? What are you doing to get there? I ask myself these questions often. They are the steerboard in my life. I will never settle for mediocrity, and neither should you.

I'm forty-three years young and have a whole nother life to live. I choose for my next forty-three to be greater than my first forty-three. I have spent forty-three years being a student of life. I'll never stop seeking knowledge and learning, but I do enjoy being a teacher: a teacher to my children, peers and those who are lost. Being a combat veteran and struggling with PTSD/PTG, I have learned a lot these past few months. When referring to "war", Thucydides says it best: "We must remember that one man is much the same as another, and that he is best who is trained in the severest school."[26] So, it's my duty to take lessons learned from being in the military and enduring all

---

[26] Thucydides. *History of the Peloponnesian War.*

my time spent on the war front and apply those to life. It's my duty to decipher those lessons and pass them along to my civilian counterparts and my family.

Too many people see a mountain, look at the top, then turn away. Why? I've climbed to the top of a few mountains. My first time, in particular, we had to use ice axes and lead lines to navigate through the snow and ice through a crevice. It was not easy and honestly, not a lot of fun at the time. But my team relied on me as I relied on the others. We were tied together. Either we all succeeded or we all failed. When we finally reached the top, the feeling was overwhelming. Maybe it was the bird's eye view of the world, the feeling of being on top of the world, the breeze or the fact that we were successful. Regardless, I became "aware" just as Anthony De Mello speaks of in his book *Awareness*. One thing I know is that it was worth it. The struggle was worth it. The fear was worth it. Those few moments when I began to lack strength and perseverance, I was quickly reminded that others were depending on me, the same way I was depending on them. You don't have to do life alone. Many people out there want you to win in life. Some people want it more than you. Maybe that's why I push people so hard. I know the feeling of great accomplishment. No drug can rival it. I want everyone to experience that feeling.

When you begin your day, feed your mind and soul with positive energy. I shared my morning routine earlier: I talk to God, read a little in whatever book I'm in, watch inspirational/motivational videos and love on my wife and kids. What is so amazing is that we're not machines. Humans are limited by nothing. No thing can stop us. We are the only limiters to what we can achieve in life. So that's why I wake up and attack the day like a lion. I choose not to be eaten in life. I choose to learn every day and win every day. Be a lion.

Every Man Should Build Something

This sounds extremely vague, I know. What I mean is every man should build with his hands in some way. The thing I recommend to most men who have hit a rut in life or just feel like they are missing something is to build a shop. I understand a lot of people don't have the space to put up a full-blown shop, but it could even be a shed or a pimped-out dog house.

After I sold my gym in November 2016, I took the proceeds and put up a shop. Now, my carpentry skills are mediocre, so I hired another combat vet to put up the structure for me. I learned a few things in the process. I sourced all the materials for the job, ordered the concrete for the pad, rented a skid steer loader and did all the dirt work myself. After the shop was built I went to the local hardware store and picked the brain of their electrician guru. Not having much experience in the whole wiring arena, I needed to know what wiring I needed to wire the outlets and lights. I found out what Romex was. The cool thing about building a shop was I had a reason to buy some new tools. I learned about internal wiring, framing, concrete, excavation, etc. After the 30×40 shop was built, I ran power to it from my main breaker in the house and buried an internet wire and added a router so I could play music, surf the web, whatever. It's basically a man cave. Occasionally I'll build some shelving, and right now, I'm about to add an upper level for more storage. I also put in a wood burning stove and learned about stove piping. All-in-all it was an absolute joy to put up.

I also recommend learning new skills.

I bought a MIG welder a couple years ago and taught myself how to weld via the University of YouTube. When I was younger, I'd play with my dad's old welder. I'd fire it up and burn through a few sticks joining pieces of metal together. I was creating. That's the whole point.

Honestly? I think we're facing an epidemic that we don't even realize is here: lack of creativity.

Think about small children. They are constantly figuring things out. I listen to my seven-year-old talk about the most outrageous things and just brush it off, but what I don't realize is that he is tapping into his creative side. As kids enter school, they are forced into a standardized curriculum. Don't even get me started on electronics! With TV, NerdPads and NerdBoxes running rampant in American households, many parents turn away from forcing their kids outside or, heaven forbid, teaching them how to use hand tools to make something. Right now, my son is asking me what he can do. He's bored. I told him to go outside and figure it out. He does this all the time, and I know how it ends. I'll go upstairs and look outside to find him building something in the dirt or with my cordless drill in the driveway screwing boards together.

As we age, we lose our creativity. With deadlines and the stress of providing an income for our families, many men don't find the time to be creative and do something out of the box. According to *Forbes*, "Prior to the 1990s, American education cultivated, inspired, and encouraged."[27] However, since then, children are losing their curiosities and passions, avoiding taking risks, avoiding collaboration, and losing imagination and deep thought due to several factors:

- Schools are narrowing students' visions by measuring their success on test scores.
- Schools are lowering expectations by focusing on students that need extra help and ignoring high-achieving students.
- Schools are narrowing students' minds by cutting back on or eliminating subjects such as social studies, science, physical education, arts, and foreign languages.
- Schools are fostering conformity by preparing students for the same tests.[28]

Find the time to build something. You can do it by yourself, with a friend or with your kids or

---

[27] Quora Contributor. "Why Our Brains Become Less Creative."
[28] Quora Contributor.

spouse, but you need to build something. Sit down and draw up the plans and work that plan. The feeling of accomplishment is outstanding! Men like building things and creating things. We were born to do it. So, do it.

Mental Fitness

I was never really one to "exercise" my brain. You see that kid who's always getting in trouble and sent into the hall? Yeah, that was me. I couldn't sit still, listening to my teachers talk for hours and hours. I've never been much of a book reader. Not unless it was loaded with pictures and came with a box of Crayons. I used to read maybe a book a year. Those books were usually non-fiction. Of course, they wanted to diagnose me with ADHD or whatever. There was nothing wrong with me. It's just the way I am wired.

It wasn't until recent years that I made a commitment to dive into the mental fitness realm. I have always considered myself a student of life. I love learning and encourage people to never stop learning. We learn in a variety of ways: 1) Tactile (touch); 2) Verbal; 3) Visual; and 4) Tech. The tech piece has been added in recent years. I'm a visual learner. If I have to sit and listen to someone talk, you can bet I'm gonna fall asleep. Honestly, I think most soldiers are like this. We learn best from practical application. That would be a mix of tactile and visual. Everyone is different. We know that. We get our creativeness from our DNA, which makes us all different.

So, how do we exercise our brains? Reading is good for us and helps us to grow. It also reignites our creative side. Because I'm a student of life and because I have chosen to exercise my mental capacity, I have read almost twenty books this past year alone. Along with reading books, I also like to watch or listen to inspiring videos on the internet. While I shower, I may fire up a daily motivation video to listen to. You gotta start your day strong. Heck! End your day strong as well. We call that "bookending," when you start your day by filling your head with positive information and doing the same before your head hits the pillow. What you think about, you will become!

Physical Fitness

No, I'm not talking about fit-ness whole pizza in my mouth. I'm talking about good, old-fashioned huffin' and puffin'. Whether it's CrossFit, powerlifting, Zumba or cycling, it doesn't matter. Get your butt moving! It's a fact that when you exert yourself, you grow. You begin to run faster, and your fast twitch muscles improve. When you run further, your endurance increases. If you lift heavier weights, your body will fight to adapt and muscle volume increases to accommodate the workload. If you stretch more often, your flexibility increases. Push yourself to that edge and maybe even beyond.

Now everyone's physical goals will differ. That's fine. Bottom line is you truly need to do something to stay active. For thousands of years, humans have been physically active. The day and age we live in now is just plain lazy. We're not walking to the next village anymore, and we don't have to plow fields by hand. I truly believe that most all illnesses we face today can be thwarted with a tall glass of physical activity. For me, I really do feel so much better after a good workout.

Along with getting physical, you need to

take your nutrition seriously. Food is an industry, and most of the food you buy is junk. Look at the labels, educate yourself and take care of that race car body you have. Hey, you've only got one and there are no do-overs. Take care of yourself. Have pride in yourself and your body. Just doing that in and of itself will motivate you to be better at everything else.

As far as nutrition goes, here's an idea for ya: fruit till noon. Weird, I know. I first heard of this while reading the book *Living with a SEAL: 31 Days Training with the Toughest Man on the Planet*. The book was given to me by my sister-in-law. I didn't pick it up for months because I thought, *Ugh! Not another SEAL book*. Come to find out, it wasn't what I thought it was going to be. Actually, it's a fantastic book! I highly recommend you get it and read it. The book is written by Jesse Itzler, a billionaire marathon, Ironman Triathlon and ultramarathon athlete entrepreneur. It highlights David Goggins, who I've come to really follow. His life story is amazing, and I often listen to him speak.

Here's the premise of eating fruit until noon by Melanie Kasper from Society Wellness:

The rules: Eat ONLY FRUIT in the morning until 12:00, and never eat fruit as part of, before or after, any other meal. The USDA recommends 2-4 servings of fruit per day. With the fruit in the morning rule, this is easily accomplished and done for the day!

In a nut shell the book looks at how the body processes and assimilates food. Fruit has the highest water content of any food, it requires less energy to digest than any other food and does not digest in the stomach with the exception of bananas, dates, and dried fruit. For this reason, making fruit your food of choice for "breakfast" (note the origin of this word; to break the fast) may be optimal. Fruit is hydrating, cleansing and detoxifying, full of vitamins, minerals, amino acids, fiber and antioxidants.[29]

I, personally, started doing it in February 2018. I was pretty strict with it for a few months. Now, I usually stick with it Monday through Friday. The first thing I noticed was how much energy I had throughout the day. The next thing I noticed was how much my bowel movements

---

[29] Melanie. "Everyday Cleanse Series."

improved. I mean, if you think about it, fruit and vegetables are water soluble, which makes them much easier to digest, decreases stress on your digestive system and increases absorption of much-needed vitamins, nutrients and minerals in your body—rather than billing your gut with protein and fats that tend to slow you down, make you feel sluggish, digest slower and are absorbed slower. Once you hit noon, game on. Eat what you wish. I can totally tell a difference in how I feel and how my digestive system feels when I eat a "hearty" breakfast in the morning. I love me some biscuits and gravy, but man, that stuff just wrecks me!

My recommendation is trying it. Commit to doing it for two weeks. See how you feel, and see if it's worth it for you. I'm a huge advocate of fruits and vegetables. I'm not anti-meat by any means. I just think it should be eaten in moderation. You'd be surprised what dialing that back would do for you. My dairy intake is extremely minimal and has been for a few years.

Spiritual Fitness

Believing in something higher than oneself

opens the gates to hope. It just makes you feel good. A major trend that is happening today, and has been happening for years, is that people dissect the Bible and pick out parts that work best for them. First of all, God didn't ask for our opinion. He made us. How in the world could we possibly know what's best for us? Second of all, He is perfect, and we are not. Now, spiritual fitness can pertain to everyone, but I am going to focus on Christianity.

Disclaimer: I am a Christian. I believe Jesus to be the son of God. I believe in the Trinity: that God, Jesus and the Holy Spirit are one. Jesus lived the life of a man on earth and never sinned. He lived a perfect life. Jesus was crucified and died on the cross to bear all mankind's sins: past, present and future. He rose from the dead three days later. Jesus was God in the flesh. God created us, the Earth and everything on and in it. He created the galaxies and stars. I believe the earth is only about six or seven thousand years old; based on doing the math of how long people lived in the Old Testament. I believe Jesus will return at a time that only God knows. Jesus doesn't even know. When he returns, all Christians, in a millisecond, will ascend with Him in the clouds and be taken to

Heaven.

Now let's get into my thoughts on making the Bible work best for you. One thing that has helped me immensely is seeking the advice and counsel of an older, wiser Christian when I question something that could be misunderstood or is questionable. Also, pray. I still have issues trying to understand what something in the Bible is trying to tell me. Most the time, I just ask my wife. She's very educated in those things. If she doesn't know, I'll ask my father or father-in-law or other Christian men and women I associate with. It's not easy living life in a Godly way. The Bible even tells us we'll have struggles. Hey, look at the Apostle Paul. That dude struggled! Just know that struggles are good. God wants us to lean into Him during those struggles so we become stronger. I sure have struggled and have been learning that leaning into Him pays off big time.

If you feel a stirring in your heart that what you question is wrong in the eyes of God, it probably is. Don't try to justify it with your human mind. The evil one has a good way of perverting and twisting truth. He is the great liar and deceiver. Don't fall prey to his schemes.

"Be sober-minded; be watchful. Your adversary the devil prowls around like a roaring lion, seeking someone to devour."

—1 Peter 5:8-11 NJV

Affirmations

Joel Osteen is great when it comes to talking about affirmations. He's a great motivator! He talks about positive affirmations or positive "I ams." I once watched a video of Denzel Washington talking about the same thing. It boils down to belief. What you believe about yourself will come to fruition. Actor Grant Cardone talks about his goals. He speaks his goals as if they have already been achieved. For example, don't say, "I want to be the best player on the football team." Instead, say, "I am the best player on the football team." Speak it in present tense. When you wake up in the morning, look at yourself in the mirror and do your affirmations. Here are some examples:

1. I am worthy
2. I am strong
3. I am equipped
4. I am a leader

5. I am ready
6. I am prosperous
7. I am successful
8. I am kind
9. I am happy
10. I am loved

I've never really done this much growing up. If I did, they weren't positive. When you feel yourself getting sucked down into the pit of depression, immediately go to the "I ams." Start repeating them. Make up your own, but remember to make them positive. That's the whole point of this practice.

Quiet Time

This little goodie has been huge for me. When I say "quiet time," I mean just that. It's my time of silence. None of life's noise to distract me. No phone, no TV, no people, nothing. Many times, this time is in my office in the basement with the door closed. It's time for me to sit and reflect on where I've been and where I intend to go. Sometimes, I'll do this first thing in the morning. I wake up, take my morning supplements, go outside to feed the dogs and check on our chickens. Then I'll begin my "me" time on what we call "Mom's Trail." We have a three-acre field with a path around it that I keep mowed for us to ride dirt bikes on or walk on. I'll begin my walk on the trail smelling the air and taking in the sights of nature. This is my time for gratitude. I'll begin to speak out loud what I am grateful for. Simple things. It goes something like this:

"What an awesome morning. Thank you for the sun and the heat and light it gives. Thank you for the beautiful sunrise and all the colors. Thank you for my eyes and the ability to still see. Thank you for the birds singing and the leaves on the trees. Thank you for the grass I'm walking on. Thank you for the easy breeze blowing my way. Thank you for the smell of fresh clean Ozarks air. Thank you for where I live, my home and my property. Thank you for our pets and chickens who give us eggs. Thank you for our home and the protection it provides us. Thank you for my incredible children and the lives they've lived and the lives they are going to live. Thank you for my smokin' hot wife and her grace. Thank you for vehicles that run smoothly. Thank you for blessing our finances and our health. Thank you for my legs, arms, fingers and toes. Thank you for my brain and that I can think and operate independently. Thank you for my friends and relationships. Thank you for my parents and sisters as well as Jill's parents and family. Lord, I pray that your favor is on me and the path I walk. Please guide my feet on the path. I pray for your continued blessings and that you would doubly bless us. I pray for wisdom and discernment. Please help me to make good decisions. Thank you for my struggles, challenges and experiences."

This quiet time of mine is to speak then listen. It's amazing how it fills my soul and guides me through the day. We have so much to be grateful for, people. I encourage you to practice taking five to ten minutes each morning to just sit and think about what you're grateful for. You may think you have it bad. Just remember, someone else has it worse.

Outer Peace Will Not Give You Inner Peace

Psalm 32:8 NJV says, "I will instruct you and teach you in the way you should go; I will counsel you with my loving eye on you." Whether you believe in what is written in the Bible or not, that's on you and may have heavy consequences someday. Regardless, what you do in life, physically and outwardly, to satisfy your thirst for peace may all be done in vain. Many people choose work, money, travel, sex, drugs, alcohol, gambling or adventure to fill them with that peace. The funny thing is, once you have peace on the inside, those external acts will become unnecessary. That doesn't mean you have to stop doing the things you enjoy, but they are just unneeded. Basically, once you have peace on the inside, you don't have to do anything to fill your peace tank. Jumping from one activity or habit to another will wear you down. You can do that, but your peace tank will still be empty. That's an issue that many combat soldier with PTSD struggle with: finding that peace. The process doesn't have to be a long process at first, but it is a lifestyle that must be practiced or that peace can fade and internal destruction and sadness can take over once again. This doesn't only relate to combat veterans but to people who are "lost" in everyday life as well. For me, I use techniques or practices that I have learned to deal with unsettling situations.

First of all, I have peace inside simply

because I wholeheartedly believe in The Trinity. That's right, the Father, the Son and the Holy Spirit. I believe in God. I believe that if I die right now, I know where I'm going: Heaven. That gives me peace. You may not believe the same, and I won't judge. I was born and raised in church, so I have those beliefs deeply rooted in me. Now I'm forty-three and continue to attend regularly with my family. So, being a believer and follower of Christ, first and foremost, gives me peace. But I also do things, daily, that help to give me peace in times of stress.

I've been subjected to some pretty gnarly stuff in my life. I've experienced and seen some crazy things. That being said, it takes quite a bit to ruffle my feathers. In the past, I've always just reacted because that's how soldiers are trained. Now, I practice not reacting but with responding using my mind and heart. Having a gun jammed into my face or someone shooting at me will get my attention, but I won't lose my composure because I've experienced that. If that happened now, I'd simply start off by taking my "4, 7, 8." That's my breathing; in for 4, hold for 7 and out for 8. That would allow me some time to create some space between me and the situation.

Along with my breathing, I practice meditation. Yeah, that's right. I was taught meditation. It has helped me immensely! That doesn't mean I'm some Buddha worshipping, cow-loving dude, and I'm not praying or giving a sacrifice to some god. Meditation just gives me my time to clear out trash from my thoughts and to clear my head. I've been able to think much more clearly and stay calmer through my daily walk. I can always tell when I've missed a practice session cause I get all bound up and tense. It is a huge relief to me, and I know my family can tell when I've done it because I'm pretty mellow. The first time I did it was kinda weird, but after my first couple, I could actually see color more brightly, smell more powerfully and love people harder. Coming from a world that is filled with nothing but grey colors, it's pretty liberating.

I have learned to stop judging people. That is another relief. I still give people the "once over" when approaching or dealing with people, but I don't let things bother me as much as I used to. When I used to see a kid with long hair, an eyebrow piercing and pants around their butt, I'd think, *Pull your freakin' pants up and clean up your act or you'll never amount to anything you stupid punk kid.*

But everyone has a story; we just don't know it until we connect with them and learn their story. Being vigilant and "profiling" is different. But judging people you come into contact with daily is a downward spiral that leads to hate and anger. Everyone deserves the benefit of the doubt. I don't see color or people's skin. I just see people. There is only one race and that is the human race, just like there are many kinds of fruits. Apples, oranges and grapes are all fruits. They are not individually different fruits. They're all still fruit. We are all God's children. Brothers and sisters. People are people and everyone deserves to be treated with the same respect. That's not to say that a decision can be made about them in the first five seconds. Just remember to try to love people in general. Doing that has made life so much more enjoyable to me.

There it is, folks! Once you find that inner peace, seeking outward peace is a waste of time. Outward activities just become hobbies. Life just happens, and it's much more enjoyable.

SUCCESS! What and How?

When talking about success and happiness, Viktor Frankl, neurologist and psychiatrist, said it best in his top-selling book *Man's Search for Meaning*:

> Don't aim at success. The more you aim at it and make it a target, the more you are going to miss it. For success, like happiness, cannot be pursued; it must ensue, and it only does so as the unintended side effect of one's personal dedication to a cause greater than oneself or as the by-product of one's surrender to a person other than oneself.[30]

There are many definitions of success. I did a survey not long ago on Facebook asking people what their definition of success was. Some people believe success is based on wealth, friends, size of family, property owned, social following, etc. To me, it's based on wins. Each day, I like to think about my wins of the day. See, I define success as doing better today than I did yesterday. If I failed at something yesterday but learned from it, that is a success because I learned something new. It's that

---

[30] Frankl. *Man's Search for Meaning*.

simple to me. I don't overwhelm myself with man-made things or material things. I simply want to continue to be better every day.

Many folks beat themselves up trying to figure out why they're not successful, but that goes back to the first paragraph. What is success to you? If you make it this ginormous mountain, good luck making the climb! Keep it simple. It's all about the wins. Winning builds confidence. I've said before that losing is a habit and so is winning. Winning each day by doing a little better than you did before becomes a habit, builds confidence and fills you with joy. It's a mindset, much like muscle memory. "When you repeat mistakes again and again, you build a muscle memory with those mistakes."[31] The same applies to winning, which leads to success. Keep it simple, and don't set yourself up for failure.

Why aren't you successful? Have you asked yourself that question? Much of it lies within what influences you directly. First of all, your social circle and activities. I like to tell people that I'm like a ship. Ships were made to sail, not sit in the port. When I decided to sail, I was off to a slow start

---

[31] Dachis. "How Muscle Memory Works."

because I had quite a few anchors attached to me. I had to cut those anchors. Another thing to think about is how you spend your time. Most people will say, "I don't have time to read." You're stating a priority, not a fact. If I told you I'd pay you ten grand to read one book in thirty days, you'd read that book. Did your priorities just change? You bet they did. What's more important to you? Those TV series you've been watching or doing better today than yesterday? I'm a huge advocate of reading books that fill me with knowledge. Here are a few I recommend:

- *Man's Search for Meaning* by Viktor Frankl

- *Awareness* by Anthony De Mello

- *The Compound Effect* by Darren Hardy

- *Dare to Dream and Work to Win* by Dr. Tom Barrett

- *Struggle Well* by Ken Falke and Josh Goldberg

Vision casting is huge. Envision yourself six months, one year or even five years from now. Where are you? What are you doing? Who are you doing it with? Think about that often. Set some goals to achieve those dreams, and write down action steps to get there. You may be doing this on your own if you haven't "pruned" negative influences out of your life. Many successful people pay other successful people to be mentors or accountability partners. Being accountable for your wins and losses will help you grow. Confess your failures to others. Journal or write things down. There is an entire world of profound knowledge out there, but you must resource the knowledge and chase it! Remember, failing is OK as long as you've learned something from it.

"Life's a garden. Dig it."[32]

– Joe Dirt

Leadership

This morning, I met a friend, Jay, for coffee. The topic of our conversation was leadership and personal growth. We were acquaintances when we met this morning, but now I'd like to call us friends. The common bond we share is that we are both veterans. Both of us had served in the Army,

---

[32] D. Tudor. "Life's garden. DIG IT Joe Dirt."

so our conversation orbited around Army leadership. Both of us were NCOs (Non-Commissioned Officers), retired as E7 Sergeants First Class, and spent time in a "schoolhouse." When I say schoolhouse, I'm referring to the Army's TRADOC (Training and Doctrine Command). If a soldier attends any schooling while serving, they attend a TRADOC course. In the civilian world, you could refer to it as college or tech school.

Since both he and I were Army instructors, we have been involved with Senior Sergeant courses. I made the comment that what's interesting is that all great modern military leaders were taught leadership by NCOs. General Mattis, General Schwarzkopf, General Franks, and General McMaster all attended courses where the classes were taught by a Sergeant. Why? Because Sergeants are the SMEs (Subject Matter Experts) in GSD or Getting Shit Done. While we attend Primary, Advanced and Senior leadership schools ourselves, we are forced into leadership roles. We have all been leaders at some point in our careers. Good or bad, we led. We were directly responsible for young lives as well as our own.

My friend and I also discussed the Army

Values. I remember during General Shinseki's reign as the Army Chief of Staff, the Army Values were pushed out Army-wide. We had a tag to wear on our dog tags as well as an Army Values card. The Army Values were an acronym, LDRSHIP. I'm sure you can see it, "Leadership." They stood for Loyalty, Duty, Respect, Selfless Service, Honor, Integrity and Personal Sacrifice. Those were drilled into us, and to this day, I still remember them and try to live by them.

The Army's definition of leadership is "the process of influencing others to accomplish a mission by providing purpose, direction, and motivation."[33] Jay and I talked about this a bit. We discussed how "motivation" is crap. Anyone can be motivated, but without action, it's worthless. Then we went on to discuss how to teach this to the civilian sector.

We were taught the 3 Leadership Styles: Delegating, Participating and Directing. Each style may be a part of someone's personality, but a good NCO should be a chameleon. Certain situations will dictate the type of leadership required at a given time. Me? I tend to lean more on the

---

[33] "Chapter 1: A Concept of Leadership."

"Participating" style. I like to be in the trench with my troops. That falls under the "Be" of the phrase "BE-KNOW-DO." I like to BE the example or set the example or bar.

Strive to follow these eleven Army Leadership Principles, and you'll do alright. If you're a leader, in the military or in the civilian sector, write these down and post them up:

- Know yourself and seek self-improvement

- Be technically and tactically proficient

- Seek responsibility and take responsibility for your actions

- Make sound and timely decisions

- Set the example

- Know your soldiers and look out for their well-being

- Keep your subordinates informed

- Develop a sense of responsibility in your subordinates

- Ensure the task is understood, supervised, and accomplished

- Build the team

- Employ your unit in accordance with its capabilities[34]

4 Leadership Principles You Must Possess

Way back when I was a young E4 studying for the E5 Sergeant Board, many things were drilled into my head. I spent every waking hour studying for the board. Military leadership has been replicated throughout the civilian sector for years, mainly due to the fact that what is done in the military has life-altering actions. If you take what works in the military, one has to believe it'll work in the civilian world. Among things learned like "BE-KNOW-DO," "Seek responsibility and accept responsibility for your actions," and the styles of leadership, one thing that has always jumped out at me was the 4 C's of Leadership: Courage, Candor, Competence and Commitment.

Courage

Courage comes in two forms. Physical courage is overcoming fears of bodily harm

---

[34] Deierlein. "11 Timeless Principles of Leadership."

and doing your duty. Moral courage is overcoming fears of other than bodily harm while doing what ought to be done. Moral courage is as important as physical courage. It is the courage to stand firm on your values, your moral principles, and your convictions. You show moral courage when you do something based on one of your values or moral principles, knowing that the action may not be in your best interest. It takes special courage to support unpopular decisions and to make it difficult for others to do the wrong thing. Others may encourage you to embrace a "slightly" unethical solution as the easiest or most convenient method. Do not ease the way for others to do wrong; stand up for your beliefs and what you know is right. Do not compromise your professional ethic or your individual values and moral principles. If you believe you are right after sober and considered judgment, hold your position.

Candor

Candor is being frank, open, honest, and sincere with your soldiers, seniors, and peers. It is an expression of personal integrity. If handled properly, disagreeing with others and presenting your point of view are not wrong. Remember these three important points: (1) select the right time and place to offer your criticism or advice; (2) do not criticize a plan without giving a constructive alternative; (3) recognize that when your leader has made the final decision, you must end your discussion and support legal and proper orders even if you do not personally agree with them. There is often no time in combat to verify reports or to question the accuracy of information. Consequences are too important, and time is too short to communicate anything but the truth. Candor is equally important in peacetime. Demand it from your subordinates and expect it from your peers and superiors. Candor expresses personal integrity.

The beliefs of a leader impact directly on the leadership climate, cohesion, discipline, training, and combat effectiveness of a unit.

Competence

Competence is proficiency in required

professional knowledge, judgment, and skills. Each leader must have it to train and to develop a cohesive, disciplined unit with all the required individual and collective skills to win on the battlefield. Competence builds confidence in one's self and one's unit; both are crucial elements of morale, courage, and, ultimately, success on the battlefield.

Commitment

Commitment means the dedication to carry out all unit missions and to serve the values of the country, the Army, and the unit. This is shown by doing your best to contribute to the Army, to train and develop your unit, and to help your soldiers develop professionally and personally.[35]

These are not principles that can be faked. They must be lived in everything you do. Many people may stray from you as you begin to practice these. That's OK because you don't want them around anyway. Good leaders can lead and be led, period. Practice these principles in everything you

---

[35] "Military Leadership."

do, and I promise you will reap the harvest.

Chapter 4: What's Wrong with My Eyes?

A Work in Progress and Crushing Life!

To start off, let's back up a few years. Like twenty-five years or so. Growing up in a home with a loving mother and father is where it began for me. Things were normal with my two sisters and my folks. My "more active negative tendencies" began in high school. I'm not really sure what it was that led me down the path, but I just started to enjoy physical confrontations. What really spurred it for me was an event that happened to me at summer camp right after my freshman year in high school in 1990. I'll be vague, but I got into a fight with another boy who was much larger than me. The fight involved a knife, lots of blood and an all-expenses paid trip to county jail for the evening. This was also my first interaction with an angel. Weird, I know.

When I arrived at the jail, they put me into the drunk tank with another guy, an older man with a torn up red shirt, dirty blue jeans and no shoes. They arrested him on the lake for intoxication. He began to give me a speech about how I'd better clean up my act or I'd end up like him. This was my first, not last, time in jail. Shortly after his speech to me, they came and got me from the cell and moved me to an office where I waited for the camp staff to come pick me up.

It wasn't until about seven years ago that this story resurfaced in my life. My dad was approached by an old friend, Mike, who was there the night at the jail. Mike was there to pick me up and sit with me during the questioning. He approached my dad about seven years ago and asked him, "Did Bryan ever mention talking to another man when he was at the jail back in 1990?" Dad wasn't really sure but continued to listen. Mike then told my dad that I went on and on about the man in the drunk tank with me. Then Mike said, "Steve, there was no one in there with Bryan the entire night. Since he was a minor, they kept him separated." To this day, I can still see that long-haired scrubby old man. The man that never existed. Mike told my dad that it had to have been an angel. Good bumps, yet? You never know when you may cross paths with an angel. It happens more than you think.

Life went on for me with some other peculiar events in my life. As I grew up and through my experiences in the military and multiple combat deployments, I continued to move with the tides of life; getting pushed to and fro. While in Iraq in 2003, my team and I had more than a couple divine interventions. Moments that should've probably killed us. Simple things like taking an alternate route to a location for some unexplained reason, then finding out later that the unit behind us went the original route and got hit.

This always upset me because I was starving for "action"! I wanted to get into it! It finally happened to me years later while in Afghanistan. In the times I've spent on combat deployments, I've seen people get killed due to different reasons. I've been around blood and that very distinct smell it has. I've had bullet *whiz* and *snap* past my head. Who needs drugs when you have combat?

That's the problem some combat vets get into it. See, once you experience that high, you want it again and again. Some people turn away from the experience and never want to experience it again, and some can't stand to be away from it. Call it a bloodlust or whatever, but it's real. Honestly, for me personally, I love a good engagement. Nothing will make you feel so alive. The only time I was honestly scared, because for a moment I thought about the kids and wife I was about to leave forever, was when I had an Afghan pointing his RPK about a foot from my head, off safe, finger on the trigger. I looked at him and thought, "Wellllll shit. This is it. FUCK!!!!!" I was so pissed off, then cooled down and was willing to accept my fate. Our QRF (Quick Reaction Force) came to the rescue, and we were able to get out of that one.

I've had many circumstances and dealings with death. It's the hate, the anger, the rage that fueled me. I struggled with it for many, many years. It affected my life with my kids, my wife and society. It was one of the main reasons for closing my CrossFit gym after six years. I just hated people, period. It wasn't until a brother of mine introduced me to BCR, a small place in Bluemont, Virginia, for combat veterans only. He and I had the same feelings about life, then he went all lovey-dovey on me. Something had changed. He invited me to attend. Against my own feelings, I accepted because I fully trusted him and knew something in my life had to change. While there, I experienced emotional warfare so deeply that every evening I was wiped out. The spiritual side was hammering away at me, and I knew God was doing something. I felt like a piece of iron being bent against my own will.

Upon completion and my arrival back home, I was pleased with being able to see color again, to smell again and to feel again. I cried probably twice a day while at BCR. It was a release that I hadn't felt since I was a child. After I was home for a few weeks, my son said, "You're weird" and laughed. I laughed as well. I was happy with this new weird. I was relieved. See, I had "unpacked my ruck," finally. My life had changed.

Don't get me wrong, I would still love to get back to the war, but I'm fine being home. My family life has changed immensely, and I actually like people. Correction, I actually *love* people. I'm diggin' life and what the future holds for me. I know there are many veterans out there struggling. I want to help. Through learning meditation and learning how to "respond" vs "react" has been huge for me. In the military, we are trained how to react constantly. We will never lose or forget our training, but as we grow, we learn to harness experience and training and then decide what is necessary for each situation. I'm working on "me." No, I'm working on "I." It has been quite a journey, and I love every minute of it. I think on a daily basis about Iraq, Afghanistan, Pakistan, The West Bank, Kosovo and other places I've been. I'll see, smell or taste something that takes me back. It's OK, though.

To those of you out there who are struggling, there is hope. Don't ever quit. Don't ever give up. Continue to fight the fight. Surround yourselves with winners and positive people. Hell, reach out to me. Find a passion to chase and continue to help others in a non-combat role. I recently got involved in a health and wellness company that is absolutely changing people's lives. It has helped me tremendously, with my health and financially. I've found that writing is therapeutic for me, and I thoroughly enjoy it.

Stop Sprinting!

This morning, we woke up to an eight-year-old son. Eight years ago, my wife was in labor giving birth just past midnight on the 12th. We have four kids. Our oldest is my twenty-year-old daughter who will be getting married in a couple weeks. My eighteen-year-old son just graduated from high school in May. The sixteen-year-old boy is driving and doing the high school thang. Then we have the youngster. Being forty-three and having lived a pretty darn full life, I have much to reflect on when days like this roll around. I also have some wisdom to share: stop sprinting. What I mean by that is cherish each moment of each day. As you age, you'll tend to slow your roll and smell the roses more. You'll look back on life and think about how fast you've run to get where you are now. Was it worth it? My wife re-posted this post by Misty Brewer Lee on her Facebook this morning, and it kinda put a frog in my throat as I read the truth that stands behind it:

> When you first have children, they talk about the challenges of parenting...the struggles of a baby waking in the night, the

toddler who won't stay in their bed, the cost of childcare, injuries from sports…Having to take off work to pick them up from school when they don't feel well, helping them with homework, a messy house, the never-ending laundry, the cost to buy school clothes, packing their lunches…You watch their eyes light up on Christmas morning…and try to soak in the magic of those moments. You coach them in sports, rushing to practices and ballgames…and tote them all over the country to let them play the game they love…no matter how exhausting or expensive it becomes. Life is just so busy that you rarely even stop to think what the end of those days look like.

In fact, it's not really even something you can wrap your mind around.

You go into it thinking that 18-20 years sounds like a long time…Then suddenly hours turn into days…days into months…and months into years. That little person that used to crawl up next to you in bed and cuddle up to watch cartoons…suddenly becomes this young adult who hugs you in the hallway as they come and go. And the chaos and laughter that used to echo throughout your home…gets filled with silence and solitude.

You've learned how to parent a child who needs you to care for and protect them…but have no clue how the whole "letting go" thing is supposed to work. So you hold on as tight as you can…wondering how time passed so quickly…feeling guilty that you missed something…Because even though you had 20 years…it just somehow doesn't seem like it was enough.

You ask yourself so many questions…

Did you teach them the right lessons?
Did you read them enough books as a child?
Spend enough time playing with them?
How many school parties did you have to miss?
Do they really know how much you love them?
What could I have done better as a parent?

…When it's time for them to go, it all hits you like a ton of bricks. And all you can do is pray…hope…and trust that God will protect them as they start to make their way into the world alone.

Parenting is by far the most amazing experience of your life...that at times leaves you exhilarated...while others leave you heartbroken. But one thing is certain...it's never enough time...

So, for all the parents with young children...whose days are spent trying to figure out how to make it through the madness...Exhausted day in and day out...

Soak. It. All. In.

Because one day...all those crazy days full of cartoons, snuggles, sleepovers, Christmas morning magic, ballgames, practices and late-night dinners...All come to an end. And you're left hoping that you did enough right, so that when they spread their wings...

They'll fly...[36]

I've traveled a lot in my life being in the Army, working for Uncle Sugar and for pleasure. I

---

[36] Misty Brewer Lee Facebook Page

sprinted so much trying to ensure that we would be taken care of financially. As I look back now, I think about all the teaching moments I've missed with my kids.

A couple years ago, my daughter said something to me that I'll never forget. She was spot on, and it radically changed my path in life. She was probably eighteen or so and had an issue with something. I was surprised that she didn't know how to overcome it, and I said, "I'm sorry. I thought I taught you how to do that." She looked at me and said, "It's alright, Dad. You were never around much anyway." Talk about a punch in the gut!

I know a lot of guys who are running around the world protecting American interests and defending our way of life. That's very honorable and very selfless. Many of those same guys have young kids at home. I feel a bit sad for them because they are walking the same path I walked. One day, their kids will be grown and moving out of the house. They'll stand there, watch their kid pull out of the driveway, scratch their head and think to themselves, *What the hell just happened?* They'll be gone and whatever tools you put in their toolbox of life is what they'll have to work with. Be it many tools or only one or two. Keep that in mind. This life absolutely blows by! We are not what's important. It's our legacy, our kids, how we train them and the tools we give them to go out and do life.

The point is this: shut off the TV in the evenings and spend that time getting to know your kids, heck, and your spouse! It's OK to have that "me time" and go golfing, hiking, shooting or whatever with your friends. You deserve it. It's also OK to include your kids. Teach them what fellowship with good people is. The bar scene? Yeah, biggest waste of money ever. Been there, done that, have the scars. That time and money could be spent investing in deeper relationships with those who really matter.

Remember that how we train our children is how they will train our grandchildren. If you neglect them, they'll neglect their own. If you invest in them and spend time with them, they'll do the same to their own. You are creating a legacy every day, good or bad, and it's making lifelong impressions on your little ones.

It's never too late to make a course correction and adjust fire. I'm forty-three, and my course correction was just a couple years ago. Better late than never.

Dads and Their Boys

Reading about fatherhood this morning in *The Way of the Wild Heart* by John Eldredge. While reading, I am thinking about how blessed I am to have my boys. I have three. My little princess is not so little anymore. She's nineteen. I read Eldredge's book *Wild at Heart* about ten years ago. Well, most of it. I need to go back and reread it. These are both great books for men to read, especially fathers. Mothers should actually read them, too, to understand men.

Having three boys is a real hoot. My seventeen-year-old is the Alpha of the three. He plays football, the chicks dig him, he's the same size as me and he's your "typical" teenage boy. My fifteen-year-old is the brainy one. He wants to be a robotics engineer. He mines crypto currency in his bedroom with a few laptops and a desktop he built himself. My six-year-old is a mix of the older two. He's inquisitive about all things, likes to take things apart and build, but he also likes to punch, run through the woods barefoot, shoot guns and wrestle. I couldn't be happier with the diversity we have in our home. My wife truly is Wonder Woman to put up with her three boys and one large boy.

Reading *The Way of the Wild Heart*, I am reminded of my own childhood and my relationship with my father. I am reminded of how important it is for fathers to "be present" in their child's lives. Especially boys and their dads. Boys need their mom to learn the velvet side of life: how to have mercy, be tender, use deodorant and take showers. But the father is the one who trains the young warriors of the house. Being a man of steel and velvet is something I strive for. My dad gave me that book decades ago, and I've never forgotten it, even though I haven't practiced it until the past year.

As boys, we love to watch our dads. We love to watch our dad's hands working a craft of some sort. I used to sit on the front porch with my Grandpa Ralph and whittle twigs with him. He gave me my first pocket knife that I still have to this day. He helped me choose the right stick and taught me how to shave away from me to create a little spear. See, our family of Hoods has a rich history of farmers and working men. I used to think that the hands of the Hood men were HUGE! I'd watch my grandpa and his brothers tie bags of fescue seed when they'd all come together to harvest it with their big shiny Gleaner combines. Those were the best days. My dad and his brothers would be out there as well. I remember climbing in the hopper of one of those big ol' combines to swim in the seeds with my cousin. It was all about the togetherness and the adventure.

Now, I'm not perfect, and I still have my moments when "I'm really busy." I hate that, but boys need to learn patience, too. Boys tend to emulate their fathers. At least that's what is natural. Boys yearn for our love and acceptance. Boys want to learn from us and want to be big and strong like us. I've spent so much time away from my children when they were younger. That's my biggest regret. I was traveling around the world doing Army stuff and working in the private sector. I've spent so much time in the field training for war. I always thought to myself, *I'm doing what I love, and I'm providing for my family*. Well, that came at a price.

For me, I choose to end it with me. My dad was gone a lot while I was growing up. He was a great dad, but he was doing what so many men do.

He traveled and worked to provide for us. Looking back, however, I think I'd rather have been without certain things just to have him around more. I didn't think about it much at the time, but I think about it now as I look back at all the ball games he missed. I try to spend as much time with him as possible, and I enjoy the moments we have together.

Men, we have one shot in life on this rock. Make it count. Create that legacy for your children. Even if you feel you don't have time for those quick moments when your son wants to show you something he built, make that time. Young men and boys seek our acceptance as fathers. They want to show us what they did or what they can do. Give them an audience. If you're an unskilled father, that's fine. Go learn those skills with your son. Take a class together; learn to do things together. We are teaching, raising and guiding tomorrow's leaders. Our boys need us.

"Be the change that you wish to see in the world."[37]

— Mahatma Gandhi

---

[37] Goodreads. "Mahatma Gandhi Quotes."

Key to Happiness?

Quality relationships with people are so important to our society. People tend to sprint through this life thinking there is some big finish for them. Yeah, death. Those people miss out on watching their kids grow; growing in their relationship with their spouse; spending time with grandparents and older, more wiser family members; and missing out on potential relationships. Opportunities are missed along the way as well. Connecting with people, I've found, is the most important thing in life. You've heard people say, "You can't take it with you when you die." Material things are not important, things such as wealth and fame. Those should only happen as a byproduct of your walk along the path.

Appreciate strangers and those you cross paths with. Smile and greet people. You'll find that not only do you make their day brighter, you'll fill your "joy tank" as well. Most people can't see past the tip of their nose and sprint through life with blinders on. Rip the blinders off, slow down and look ahead. It's not about you. It's about the legacy we create for future generations. What are we

131

teaching our kids and the youth in our society? It's OK to be kind to people, and it's not a sign of weakness. I like to think about the ancient Shaolin Monks or the Asian culture: extremely honorable, living a life of service to others and/or a higher being. They are tremendously disciplined in their practices and with their tools, be it weapons or those in another trade.[38]

I'm a believer, a Christian. I believe God created Adam in His own image and then created Eve. God's perfect design is that of a team and for people to have a relationship with others. People's religions, the color of skin, sex, sexual preference or any other debatable trait should not matter. We are all in this thing called life together. We all struggle, and we all have a story. No one person is better than another. Humility is massive! Strive to meet new people and learn about them. One of the greatest things I've done for myself was to get into Network Marketing. It forced me to meet new people, smile and listen to their stories. Because I'm a man of honor and not a shyster, I believe in getting to know people so I can serve them best.

---

[38] Szczepanski. "The Shaolin Monks."

Feelings

Just saying the word "feelings" makes me feel a little uneasy. You gotta understand, for someone like me to have those, it almost makes me feel soft. I've learned that it's OK and it's natural. Being in the military, I don't remember getting issued feelings. In fact, I learned on day one that my feelings don't matter. If the Drill Sergeant wanted to know how I felt, he'd tell me. You learn to suppress those. Why? Because on the battlefield, we ain't got time for feelings. You have to be decisive without being emotional. As I look back now, joy began to leave me in high school. The last time I truly had joy in my heart was probably junior high school. As we watch at the teen suicide rate rise, we can't but wonder why. According to Kidsdata.org, youth suicide and self-harm are important topics for several reasons:

> Suicide is the second leading cause of death among young people ages 15-24 in the U.S. A nationwide survey in 2015 found that more than 1 in 6 high school students reported seriously considering suicide in the previous year, and more than 1 in 12 reported attempting it. In addition, approximately 157,000 youth ages 10-24 are

treated for self-inflicted injuries in emergency rooms every year. Self-inflicted injuries are not necessarily the result of suicide attempts; in fact, self-harm without the intent to die is more prevalent than self-harm with such intent. Across all ages, suicide and self-inflicted injury in the U.S. cost an estimated $45 billion annually in medical expenses and work loss; actual costs may be higher as many suicides and attempted suicides are not reported due to social stigma.

Some groups are at a higher risk for suicide than others. Males are more likely than females to commit suicide, but females are more likely to report attempting suicide. Among racial/ethnic groups with data, American Indian/Alaska Native youth have the highest suicide rates. Research also shows that lesbian, gay, and bisexual youth are more likely to engage in suicidal behavior than their heterosexual peers. Several other factors put teens at risk for suicide, including a family history of suicide, past suicide attempts, mental illness, substance abuse, stressful life events, low levels of communication with parents, access to lethal means, exposure to suicidal behavior of others, and incarceration.[39]

I actually attempted suicide in high school. Yep, I'm a statistic. At the time, my girlfriend had broken up with me. She started seeing another guy, and it infuriated me! I needed her attention, and I was sad. So, I took a bunch of my parents' pills, drove in my car to an empty parking lot, took about seventy-five pills and filled my belly with water. I sat back and cried. My life literally began to flash before me. I felt this voice screaming at me, "GO TO THE HOSPITAL NOW!" Looking back, I'm not even sure I was in control of my body. I started my car and drove directly to the hospital. When I arrived at the emergency room, I told them what I had done, and they began to pump my stomach and make me drink the charcoal stuff. They called my mom, and she came to the ER. My dad was out of town for work. Looking back now, I can only think of the saying, "You ain't dead yet cause God ain't done with you."

I think we can all agree, looking back, that high school was a challenging time in our lives. As

---

[39] Kidsdata.org. "Self-Inflicted Injury Hospitalizations."

hormones dump into our system, the young bulls position themselves for a place in the pasture. We care too much about what other people think vs what really matters. Therefore, our feelings are bottled up. This is not healthy, and it is not normal. Coming full circle and having my heart come back online and feeling joy in my life again, it just frustrates me what is happening with our youth. You know what? It's OK to have feelings. We are born with them like arms and legs. They are part of us. They are the most important part of us. Fear and sadness are as normal as joy. We also feed the feelings we choose. That's why I've chosen to do things and surround myself with things that bring me joy.

I look at it like this: we begin each day with a pocket of "Joy Bucks." As I go throughout my day, I choose what I want to spend my Joy Bucks on. They are mine, and no one can take my Joy. I surrender them when I choose. It is a physical impossibility for someone to make me mad. No, I choose anger. I can be a duck and let it roll off, or I can engage. I can react. People aren't understood. That gives them the feelings of anger and sadness. Fear of loss, maybe. Fear of hopelessness, maybe. Choose joy. Choose to be a duck. You own your feelings. No one can take them from you.

Remember that we are born with three primary feelings: joy, fear and sadness. Think about it. Watch babies. Like primary colors, you can mix those feelings to create another feeling.

Joy + Fear = Excitement

Fear + Sadness = Anger

Then, mix those secondary feelings with primary or other secondary feelings, and you get all sorts of feelings.

According to Jim JP Collins, host of *The Anxiety Podcast*, the difference between anxiety and excitement is our interpretation.[40] Combat vets with PTSD experience anxiety in large crowds, mostly because of their association between being in an open space with a bunch of people and the chaos of war or gunfights or IEDs going off. If a person is able to realize that a past experience is something that happened and is not guaranteed to happen again, that alone could reduce the anxiety they feel. Same goes for females who've been sexually abused. They may have anxiety when engaging in

---

[40] Lennon. "Are Anxiety and Excitement."

a sexual activity with their spouse because of what happened in the past. They felt unsafe then and naturally feel unsafe now. Through choice, they can change that. Disclosure could be of great help and knowing that nothing is wrong with them. Instead, something happened.

Feelings are weird and are the main driver of our behavior. Learning to respond vs react and practicing that will have great desirable effects on a person's life. In the Army, we were always taught to react. Sight and action. Now that I've been taught to involve my heart and have congruency with my mind and heart, the actions I choose are more positive. Learning to understand a person or situation then following your heart will increase the likelihood of a positive outcome. Key word there is "understand." Always seek understanding before making decisions.

Chapter 5: Faith

Epiphany in the Amazon—Realizing Your Purpose

I recently went on a mission trip to the Amazon Rainforest. We flew into Manaus, Brazil, to stay the night, then headed up the Rio Negro river the next day. Our boat ride was about five peaceful hours skimming along the water of that amazing place. We were there to build church number 95 of 100. The first day of work would be the next day. Everyone was so excited to get to shore, meet the people and kids of the village and get to work! All twenty-two of us went to shore that morning. The weather there is a little different from anything I've experienced, and I have been all over the Middle East and a few places in Central America. We were close to the sun since we were close to the equator, on a river in their springtime. The bugs weren't bad at all, but that dagum heat was miserable. Felt like a sweaty fat man was on me constantly.

That first day, Monday, would be the true test for those who hadn't ventured out much in the world. We had a few heat casualties that day as well as one injury. The next day, I had gotten pretty sick, so I had to stay back on the boat to rest up. The third day, I was back to work, but our numbers on shore had been cut in half. On the fourth day, only four or five of us were actually working on the church. After we had gotten done, all we could accomplish for our trip, we began to clean up. One of the guys who worked side-by-side with me had a very dry sense of humor. I got it, most others didn't. That dude totally cracked me up! As part of the cleanup, we had to carry these picnic tables about 200 yards across the village. On our way, he made a comment to me, "Man, I'm kinda pissed off." I was blown away that he said the "P" word! I asked why, and he went on to tell me that he had wished more people would've come to help build so he could go on the trips to hand out water filters to nearby villagers. He and I had gone the day prior to do this. It was such a great feeling and filled me with joy to present the water filters to those people. He had made mention that it seemed it was only us doing the welding, brick work, etc. I agreed, silently, and told him, "Yeah, I get it." I thought about it for a minute and told him, "Dude, everyone is born with a purpose and everyone has gifts. No one on Earth is meant to just exist. Maybe those other people have the gift of encouragement, music, organization or whatever. God gifted us with the skills of trade labor. We have gifted hands, and we're 'get stuff done' kind of guys. I know it stinks, and I feel the same way. I'm just glad we were able to do our part on the church."

Everyone has a gift or a talent. A God-given gift. If you don't know what that gift is, here are some criteria to make you think:

1. What do you really enjoy doing?
2. Would you do what you really enjoy doing for free?
3. What is it that people tell you you're good at doing?

Chew on that for a bit. I'll bet with some

triangulation, pinpointing, you'll be able to find that common denominator. What one thing do all those questions point to? That, my friend, is more than likely your gift. What now? I implore you to lean into that gift. Use that gift for good and bless the world with your new-found talent. Lastly, thank God for blessing you with that gift.

Be, Today

My wife has encouraged me to start attending the men's Bible study at church. I know I should and it'd be good for me, but *dang*, it's at 6:00 am! Anyhow, I got up at 5:00 am this morning and attended. She's usually right 100% of the time.

The pastor leading the Bible study is a guy named Craig Groeschel. This was the first meeting of a six-week study. The main topic today was what to do, mainly about life and whatnot. I struggle with the questions "What now?" and "What do I do with my life?" Most men live life according to their identity. That identity comes from the line of work they're in. Bryan the Army guy. Bryan the contractor. Bryan the CrossFit gym owner. I've struggled with my identity for years.

Who am I, and what do I do? The pastor said it should be "Who before Do," not "What I do is who I am." That got me to thinking: Who am I, and who do I want to be?

Well, I know that I'm a child of God, husband, father, brother, son and friend. I like being all of that. Since my life has changed radically over the past year, I've let my walk be led by my heart more times than not. Who I want to be is a person who's created a legacy. I want to have raised my children right, not according to me or society, but in the eyes of the old man upstairs. I want my children to want to create a legacy. When I'm dead, I want folks to remember me as a servant to humankind, a helper, an encourager, a leader and an educator. Knowing all of that, what do I do? I've served in the Army for over twenty-five years. My wife and I talk often about getting more involved with missions, building schools or churches and helping to feed folks around the globe. That's where my heart is. I want to help people who are unable to help themselves.

The second part he discussed this morning was, "Why before What." I thought that was interesting because it brought to light our motives. Why do sales people hit the road and try to sell things? What is the motive? Well, to make money! Is there a motive behind that? I know that I want to go out into the world and help people. Well, that takes capital to do those things. I would love to buy a well digger and dig wells in Africa. Unless someone donates one to me and ships it over there, I'm going to have to buy one and ship it myself. That's going to take a lot of cash.

Now I know who I am and what my motive is. That's why I work this network marketing business. It's kind of the best of both worlds. I could care less about fancy cars, boats, etc. Not my jam. To me, it's all God's money, and he blesses us with it to be good stewards of His money. Yeah, I've blown cash on silly things, but as I grow and mature, I recognize that more. In Robert Kiyosaki's book *Rich Dad Poor Dad*, he mentions that a direct sales company is a great way to raise capital while working your regular job. That capital can be for an investment or whatever. It all kinda makes sense to me now. If your motive is good, the Why, then the source of income, the What, will be there.

The Three Fuels of Success

I used to see it all the time as a CrossFit affiliate owner, and I've seen it with my kids and many other people who begin a new adventure in life. Think about your buddy who played their first eighteen holes of golf. Remember how they went out and spent thousands of dollars on shoes, gloves, clubs, towels, balls, tees, bag and lessons? Six months later, you ask them how their game was coming along and they say, "Yeah, about that. I haven't golfed in months."

That, my friends, is what I like to call the "Bottle Rocket Effect." People start something new, and their level of enthusiasm is through the roof. But because they lacked two other fuels, they were not able to have that break through.

The three fuels people need to be successful are enthusiasm, commitment and conviction.

Enthusiasm

You probably see it the most in network marketing. People see a presentation, learn just enough about the product, think it's the best thing since pockets on shirts, and run out to tell everyone about it at full speed. After they begin to receive some push back and people telling them no, they quit. Why? They weren't committed in the first place.

The first 5K run my eighteen-year-old did with me when he was about eight I told him specifically, "Now, a lot of people are going to take off running at a sprint. Don't do that. Start with a nice jog to get into a rhythm that works for you. I'll run with you the entire time." You already know what happened. *BANG!* The gun went off, and like being chased by a hoard of zombies, he was gone. All the other kids did it as well. I just smiled and began my trot. About 150 yards later, I caught up to him. He was fading fast. As I began to pass him, I lovingly hollered, "Come on! Stay with me!" He almost vomited a few times, but as I slowed my roll, he was able to keep at a pace we could finish with.

Life, success and business is not a sprint. Heck, it's not even a 5K. It's a marathon, baby. That first fuel of enthusiasm will only take you so far. It's an awesome fuel, don't get me wrong, but it will burn out. You must have that level of commitment.

Commitment

Once the initial excitement has begun to burn out, the emotion of "Will" kicks in. Commitment takes purpose and focus. Goal setting is critical at this point, and achieving those goals are of the utmost importance. Commitment is being able to take a couple punches but stay on your feet. Being able to ride the storm knowing and believing there are sunny skies. This fuel can override thoughts or feelings of wanting to quit, coast or back off for a while. The one thing I've personally found is that if you don't truly believe in your product or service you are offering, your commitment is a pipe dream. It's a false hope. So, make sure what you are offering truly does provide value to people.

Conviction

The last fuel is the one that will get you through anything. It is unflinching belief and is non-negotiable. This faith is unshakable. For me, I have that conviction in my current business. That is what makes me smile like I know a secret others do not. It drives me! Conviction is what keeps people going when they hit a wall, start to experience fatigue and slow growth. What I have found to work best in growing my conviction is surrounding myself with other successful people who have the same conviction as I do. The cool part about that is that it will restore your enthusiasm! You become like those you associate with. Practicing this and knowing how these three fuels work is paramount to your own success.

"A 'No' uttered from the deepest conviction is better than a 'Yes' merely uttered to please, or worse, to avoid trouble."[41]

— Mahatma Ghandi

Always continue to learn and practice good habits. Emulate successful people. Those good habits will compound daily. Over time, the marathon you have been running will look like a mere 5K.

We All Walk the Path of Life

I am on a path. That path is called "Warrior PATHH," and I was introduced to this at BCR in February 2017. The path never ends, and if embraced, the path leads to understanding past

---

[41] Goodreads. "Mahatma Gandhi Quotes."

experiences and welcoming new experiences with more knowledge of self and preparation for receiving the unknown. The more a person experiences, the more a person struggles and grows. The more a person grows, the stronger and more useful they become. We know that struggle is good and is even referenced in the Bible in Romans 5:3-5 NJV.

> Not only that, but we rejoice in our sufferings, knowing that suffering produces endurance, and endurance produces character, and character produces hope, and hope does not put us to shame, because God's love has been poured into our hearts through the Holy Spirit who has been given to us.

Many people have asked me, "What's different about you? What changed?" Understanding and accepting life's experience is what changed. General Mattis summed it up best when he said, "There is also something called Posttraumatic Growth. Where you come out of a situation like that and you actually feel kinder towards your fellow man and fellow woman. That you actually are a better husband and father. You actually have a closer relationship with your

God."[42] This can relate to those parents who have lost children, experienced combat, were assaulted or attacked, had an abusive childhood, witnessed brutality or any other type of traumatic event. Most people have no idea how to process that event. Just know, we cannot choose or control those external forces, but we can choose how we respond to those forces. We choose our path.

"We all walk the same path, but got on different shoes."[43]

– Drake

For combat veterans, especially those who enlisted at a young age, we were not taught certain principles or at least were not able to exercise them. On the battlefield, there is no time to mourn. Mission first. The three principles I have chosen to relearn and put to use are Grace, Patience and Understanding. These principles allowed me to stop and take an assessment of certain situations— out of my control—and react accordingly. Here is a real-world experience of my own and is a 100% true story:

---

[42] Max. "General Mattis."
[43] AZquotes. "Drake Quote."

Seven days, to the day, prior to my attendance to BCR, my six-year-old accidentally knocked over a glass of orange juice. He was sitting at the island in our kitchen eating breakfast when I heard his plastic cup fall over. As I turned around, I saw the orange juice making its way to the edge of the island and begin to pour onto our hardwood floor like a waterfall. I ran over towards him, picked up the cup and slammed it down and yelled, "12:00 O'CLOCK! 12:00 O'CLOCK!! HOW MANY TIMES DO I HAVE TO TELL YOU?!" referring to the cup position in reference to his plate. Then I yelled, "GO TO YOUR ROOM. YOU GET NO BREAKFAST THIS MORNING!" After I cleaned up the mess, I went to his room and asked him why he was crying. He said, "Cause I'm scared." It just crushes me as I remember him running to his room crying.

Fast forward fourteen days later, and I am convinced this entire thing was a God thing. Seven days later, to the day, after my time spent at BCR, the exact same thing happened. We were in the kitchen, doing the same thing and in the same configuration. I was at the sink when I heard the cup fall over. I turned around and saw what had happened. His eyes were wide open, and I said,

"Ah, SNAP! Well, what are we going to do?" He looked at me and said, "I don't know." I said, "Well, we'd probably better clean it up. What do you think we should use to clean it up?" He said we should use a paper towel, and that's what we did, together. No voice raising, only love and grace. I strive to exercise Grace, Patience and Understanding every day because they don't issue those in Basic Training. I had to learn them all these years later.

Soldiers, typically, have high expectations and zero room for error because the slightest deviation from perfect can result in death of oneself or a comrade. This is the path I am on. No head doctor can give "tools" that will amount to much because, just like old tools in my toolbox, they can get rusty. These are skills that must be practiced daily. We are all on a path, and if you walk that path with blinders on, never seeking personal growth and development, you will run through life not having made progress. Remember, struggle is good if you do it well. Most importantly, choose well who you walk your path with.

Grace, Patience, Understanding

People ask me what has changed in my life. The foundational character principles that I walk on are major players in the transformation I have and am undergoing. These three principles couldn't be further from the mold of a soldier. When someone screws up, you discipline or punish them. No time is taken to try and *understand*, therefore no *grace* is given. There is no *patience* in trying to *understand*. It's strictly see and react.

"For by grace you have been saved through faith. And this is not your own doing; it is the gift of God."

- Ephesians 2:8 KJV

Grace

I was first impacted by grace a year ago at BCR. Growing up in a Christian home, I guess I always knew about grace, but as I moved into adulthood and moved away from my Christian upbringing, I let it all slip away. There are twenty-five verses in the Bible that reference Grace.[44] Merriam-Webster has some interesting

---

[44] Bible Study Tools Staff. "Grace Bible Verses."

definitions of Grace. To me, it's similar to forgiveness. I will always screw up, and I know other people will screw up as well. Giving mercy, approval and favor to others has helped to refill the "Joy Tank" in my life. I don't expect it, but when it's given to me, I appreciate it. It is something I have never given to my children until the recent year. You would be amazed at how much of a calming effect grace has on a person.

Patience

I have never had much patience for anything I didn't agree with. I tell people that expectations only lead to hurt feelings. If you have expectations, you must have patience or you will live in the fireball of stress and anger. People pray for patience, and God will usually give you the opportunity to learn it. Feelings, principles and skills are not just given to us. They are learned. You have to be tested to learn. If you continue to fail those tests and fail to submit and continue to fight it, you will live in defeat. Patience is a wonderful thing. We all, should, know that you have to give to get. Again, we are all human. There is no perfect person breathing the air we do. Nowhere. That being said, patience is critical to communication and harmony. Too many people lack patience in today's day. Too many people have expectations and expect others to see things as they do, believe things as they do and do things as they do. Again, hurt feelings. You want to know one of the best tools to use when tested with patience? Breathing. Just breath and know that this life is temporary. The world will not end if things do not go your way. Be like a reed in the wind, and be flexible. Patience is a true art that must be practiced. Your life will yield so much more piece once you realize that and begin to practice it.

"To lose patience is to lose the battle."[45]

— Mahatma Gandhi

Understanding

For many years, it was my way or the highway. I didn't really care about the input of others. I didn't really care to know about other people's issues. Get stuff done and don't let your personal life affect what is going on now. When people learn to control their mouth muscle and open their ears, the amount of critical data absorbed is amazing. That's why we have two ears and one mouth. Listening to people and truly

---

[45] AZquotes. "Mahatma Gandhi Quote."

working to understand them or the situation at hand will result in much more happiness than anger and confusion. Truly trying to understand people opens the door to sympathy and empathy. People need that from others. People want to be understood.

Grace, patience and understanding go hand in hand. I never practiced these three principles and never gave them to anyone because I felt they were not given to me, even if they were. God in Heaven is the only person who has given me His grace. He's been patient with me in finally coming around or in times when I have failed. I know He understands me because He created me.

CONCLUSION

My prayer is that what I have written has opened up new possibilities for you. I also hope that you feel encouraged. Maybe you've even had some chuckles reading this. I truly love people, and I love being able to connect with folks. Getting started is the hardest part. That ol' nasty dude, Fear, holds us back. It is absolutely paralyzing. Be bold! Be courageous. Take that first step. Each step you take after that will be easier. The more space you can place between you and your past, or whatever it is that's been holding you back, the easier it will be to move forward. Be positive! Surround yourself with the right people. People who'll fill you and encourage you. I believe God created one race, the human race. Yes, he blessed us with different shapes, colors and sizes of people. That's what makes us great. Reach across political party lines, ethnic backgrounds and religions. Lock arms with others. We are all on this rock doing this thing called life together. Everyone struggles. Don't be fooled. Everyone screws up. No one person is above another. We are all just regular people trying to figure it out and live the best life we can. It doesn't matter how fancy or meager you are, how much money you make or don't make, how big or small your house is, what your background is or what school you went to, what color you are or who you pray to, what neighborhood you grew up in or who your parents are. Remember, we're all still human.

Thank you so much for reading. Be a pal and encourage others to buy this book.

Bucket List Item:

Write and publish a book. Check!

Thank you to my school teachers and the men in my church youth group. Especially those who were hard on me and never gave up. You made more of an impact than you'll ever know.

Bibliography

AZquotes. "Drake Quote." AZquotes.
https://www.azquotes.com/quote/1110785.

AZquotes. "George Washington Carver Quote."
AZquotes.
https://www.azquotes.com/quote/50333.

AZquotes. "Mahatma Gandhi Quote." AZquotes.
https://www.azquotes.com/quote/649470.

Barrett, Tom. *Dare to Dream and Work to Win:
Understanding the Dollars and Sense of Success
in Network Marketing*. Vienna, VA:
Business/Life Management, 1998.

Bible Study Tools Staff. "Grace Bible Verses." Bible
Study Tools.
https://www.biblestudytools.com/.

"Chapter 1: A Concept of Leadership." *The U.S.
Army Leadership Field Manual: FM 22-100*.
Indianapolis, Ind. BN Publishing, 2008.
http://library.enlistment.us/field-
manuals/series-2/FM22_100/CH1.PDF.

D. Tudor. "Life's garden. DIG IT Joe Dirt."
YouTube video, 0:11. Posted March 9, 2013.

https://www.youtube.com/watch?v=Akec_5
zCgso.

Dachis, Adam. "How Muscle Memory Works and How It Affects Your Success." Lifehacker. May 6, 2011. https://lifehacker.com/how-muscle-memory-works-and-how-it-affects-your-success-5799234.

De Mello, Anthony. *Awareness*. Grand Rapids, Michigan: Zondervan, 1990.

Deierlein, Tom. "11 Timeless Principles of Leadership (US Army 1948)." LinkedIn. June 7, 2014. https://www.linkedin.com/pulse/201406071 31713-404673-11-timeless-principles-of-leadership-us-army-1948.

First People. "Two Wolves: A Cherokee Legend." First People. https://www.firstpeople.us/.

Fordham, Michael S.M., and Frieda Fordham. "Carl Jung." *Encyclopedia Britannica*. Encyclopedia Britannica, Inc. Published March 8, 2019. https://www.britannica.com/biography/Carl-Jung.

Frankl, Viktor E. *Man's Search for Meaning*. Beacon

Press, 2006.

Goodreads. "Carl Jung Quotes." Goodreads. https://www.goodreads.com/author/quotes/ 38285.Carl_Jung.

Goodreads. "Flannery O'Connor Quotes." Goodreads. https://www.goodreads.com/quotes/315733- i-write-because-i-don-t-know-what-i-think- until.

Goodreads. "Friedrich Nietzsche Quotes." Goodreads. https://www.goodreads.com/author/quotes/ 1938.Friedrich_Nietzsche.

Goodreads. "G.K. Chesterton Quotes." Goodreads. https://www.goodreads.com/author/quotes/ 7014283.G_K_Chesterton.

Goodreads. "Henry Ford Quotes." Goodreads. https://www.goodreads.com/author/quotes/ 203714.Henry_Ford.

Goodreads. "Joseph Campbell Quotes." Goodreads. https://www.goodreads.com/author/quotes/ 20105.Joseph_Campbell.

Goodreads. "Mahatma Gandhi Quotes."
Goodreads.
https://www.goodreads.com/author/quotes/
5810891.Mahatma_Gandhi.

Goodreads. "Mark Twain Quotes." Goodreads.
https://www.goodreads.com/author/quotes/
1244.Mark_Twain.

Hammond, Darin L. "11 Reasons Why You Need
To Be More Independent." Lifehack.
https://www.lifehack.org/articles/productivi
ty/11-reasons-why-you-need-more-
independent.html.

Kidsdata.org. "Self-Inflicted Injury
Hospitalizations." Kidsdata.org.
https://www.kidsdata.org/topic/212/self-
inflictedinjuryhospitalization-
rate/table#fmt=2397&loc=2,127,347,1763,331,
348,336,171,321,345,357,332,324,369,358,362,
360,337,327,364,356,217,353,328,354,323,352,
320,339,334,375,343,330,367,344,355,366,368,
265,349,361,4,273,59,370,326,333,322,341,338,
350,342,329,325,359,351,363,340,335&tf=79&
sortType=asc.

Lennon, Annie. "Are Anxiety and Excitement the
Same Thing?" Sutava. December 13, 2017.

https://www.sutava.com/anxiety-excitement-thing/.

Lockie, Alex. "15 Fortune 500 CEOs who got their start in the military." Business Insider. August 26, 2015. https://www.businessinsider.com/15-fortune-500-ceos-who-got-their-start-in-the-military-2015-8#verizon-lowell-mcadam-14.

Max. "General Mattis on The #1 Misperception of Veterans." YouTube video, 2:57. Posted April 9, 2015. https://www.youtube.com/watch?v=FgJascdvJ8A.

Melanie. "Everyday Cleanse Series: Fruit in the Morning, a Great Way to 'Break-Fast' and Start Your Day. Try It!" Society Wellness. June 1, 2015. http://www.societywellness.com/everyday-cleanse-series-fruit-in-the-morning-a-great-way-to-break-fast-and-start-your-day-try-it/.

"Military Leadership." *U.S. Army Leadership Manual*, FM 22-100. July, 31, 1990.

Mindfulness 360 - Center For Mindfulness. "'What

We Can Learn From Lobster About Stress' ~
Rabbi Dr. Abraham Twerski." YouTube
video, 1:14. Posted November 29, 2016.
https://www.youtube.com/watch?v=VEXIF2
hNmv8.

Misty Brewer Lee Facebook Page. Accessed 5
February, 2019.
https://www.facebook.com/misty.brewerlee
.

Morin, Greg. "Your Plan and Your Story." P1
Performance Group. June 15, 2015.
http://www.p1performancegroup.com/blog/
2015/6/15/your-plan-and-your-story.

Quora Contributor. "Why Our Brains Become Less
Creative As We Get Older." *Forbes*. August
3, 2016.
https://www.forbes.com/sites/quora/2016/08
/03/why-our-brains-become-less-creative-
as-we-get-older/#14bf0b047955.

Ramos, Catarina, and Isabel Leal. "Posttraumatic
Growth in the Aftermath of Trauma: A
Literature Review About Related Factors
and Application Contexts." *Psychology,
Community & Health* [Online], Volume 2
Number 1. March 28, 2013.

https://pch.psychopen.eu/article/view/39/ht
ml#aff1.

Robbins, Tony. "Tony Robbins – Blame Them."
Goalcast video, 1:07. Posted January 10,
2017.
https://www.goalcast.com/2017/01/10/tony-
robbins-crediting-others-success/.

Shenk, Joshua Wolf. "What Makes Us Happy?" *The
Atlantic*, June 2009 Issue (June 2009).
https://www.theatlantic.com/magazine/arch
ive/2009/06/what-makes-us-happy/307439/.

Szczepanski, Kallie. "The Shaolin Monks: Warriors
of the Chinese Monastery." ThoughtCo.
July 16, 2017.
https://www.thoughtco.com/history-of-the-
shaolin-monks-195814.

Thucydides, Rex Warner, and M. I. Finley. *History
of the Peloponnesian War*. Harmondsworth,
Eng: Penguin Books, 1972.

Wikipedia contributors. "Grant Study." *Wikipedia,
The Free Encyclopedia*, last modified
February 8, 2019.
https://en.wikipedia.org/w/index.php?title=
Special:CiteThisPage&page=Grant_Study&i

d=882394511.

Willink, Jocko, and Leif Babin. *Extreme Ownership: How U.S. Navy SEALs Lead and Win*. St. Martin's Press, 2015.

ABOUT THE AUTHOR

Bryan Hood was raised in Springfield, Missouri, where he joined the Army reserves at the age of seventeen. He knew he wanted to be a soldier since he was a small boy. As a child, you'd find him in the woods behind his house playing G.I. Joe or guns with other neighborhood kids. Spending much of his summers at the family farm, Bryan had a love for the outdoors and adventure. In his teen years, he struggled with many of the typical challenges and issues children face: poor grades, getting into fights, drinking, disagreeing with his parents, etc. Having grown up in a Christian home and attending church regularly, he knew what was right but chose "the hard way."

After enlisting for active duty at the age of nineteen, he quickly married his seventeen-year-old high school sweetheart and began life at Ft. Stewart, Georgia. He was assigned duty stations in Georgia, Virginia and Germany, and he decided to leave active duty in 2000. He then returned home to Springfield, Missouri, with his wife and two kids, where he took a job with his father in the farm equipment business. He enlisted in the Army Reserves upon leaving active duty to continue his service. In 2003, Bryan's unit was called to active duty in support of Iraqi Freedom where he served twelve months in various locations in Iraq. After returning home, he spent a month at home trying to figure out his next steps in life. A year later, he and his wife would divorce after many years of marital struggle.

About that time, he and some work mates sought out new careers in the private military sector and began contract work in war zones. Bryan took a job with a very notable company and worked for them for five years, then worked another two doing similar work for a different company. He also married his dream girl in 2006, and they had a son together in 2010. During those seven years working in the intelligence community for a government agency, he never realized how much was going on back home. His older children were growing up without him and his wife was holding down the fort with their infant son. In 2012, Bryan was injured in Kandahar in a non-combat accident, prohibiting him from ever returning to the "rock star," adrenaline-junkie lifestyle. While trying to manage the CrossFit gym he began after his injury, and several subsequent surgeries, he began to sink into depression. During this time, he struggled with anxiety, depression, survivor guilt from the loss of many friends, prior marital issues, isolation, trouble sleeping and an opiate addiction. He closed his CrossFit gym in November 2016 and told his wife he was "ready to go to heaven." About the same time, an old contracting buddy reached out to him about a combat veteran retreat and encouraged him to commit to attend. In February 2017, he did, and it changed his life.

Recently, being medically retired from the Army for PTSD and a host of other issues, Bryan has grown deeper than ever in his Christian faith. He mentors other combat veterans who struggle with PTSD. The path of Post Traumatic Growth has been amazing for Bryan but has not always been easy. He still has his struggles and has learned skills to manage and practice during those "times in the valley." Beginning a career in network marketing forced Bryan to jump back into society and meet new people, to determine how he can positively impact their lives.

Bryan can be contacted via his Facebook page.

www.facebook.com/bryanchood/

or

www.hoodlm.org

42160744R00117

Made in the USA
Lexington, KY
14 June 2019